I WAS
BLIND
(Dating),
BUT NOW
I SEE

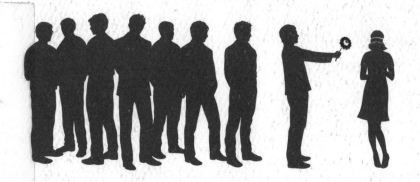

my misadventures in dating,

waiting, and stumbling into love

Stephanie Rische

If you've ever been brave enough to outright ask God for the desire of your heart only to be met with what feels like stony silence, this book is for you. Whether you've prayed for a husband or kids or dream job or healing or hope or home and haven't heard back, this book is for you. Stephanie asked and God did not answer in any of the ways he could have. Through eight blind dates, God did not change his answer. Instead he changed Stephanie. And if you read her book, I'm pretty certain he's going to change you, too.

LISA-JO BAKER

Author of *Surprised by Motherhood* and community manager for (in)Courage

In *I Was Blind (Dating), but Now I See*, Stephanie's funny, tender, and insightful words take the reader on a journey that points to God's faithfulness and kindness at every stop along the road. You'll have a blast reading this book—you'll laugh, you'll nod your head, and you may even cringe at some pretty spectacular awkward moments. More than anything, though, you'll be encouraged by the compassion and the care of our very good God. Well done, sweet Stephanie!

SOPHIE HUDSON

Author of *Home Is Where My People Are* and *A Little Salty to Cut the Sweet*

This is not just a book about dating: It's about living, about not putting your life on hold. But more important, it's about surrounding yourself with a spiritual posse—mentors, friends, prayer partners, family—who will walk with you through the valleys and around the blind corners. Stephanie Rische is one of those people: honest, hilarious, and wise. Her book is a treasure!

SARAH ARTHUR

Author of *The One Year Coffee with God* and *Dating Mr. Darcy*

I've known Stephanie Rische primarily as a fine editor, but it was fun getting to know her as a skilled and entertaining writer! Not only singles but marrieds will readily identify with this engaging book. Stephanie is refreshingly honest as she addresses, with good humor, life's awkward moments and unwelcome emotions. Her transparency, charm, and faith in Christ are magnetic. I really enjoyed this book, and highly recommend it!

RANDY ALCORN

Author of *Happiness* and *Heaven*

Finally! An honest look at the journey we call dating. With the winsomeness of a "pit bull in a tutu" (her words), Stephanie opens her heart and soul to the twists and turns, the anticipation and disappointment of this daunting endeavor. She has the courage to let us in to the parts of her world that most of us work hard to keep hidden, and that is the best gift of all.

NANCY ORTBERG

Author of *Seeing in the Dark*

If you're struggling to hope that you will ever find "Mr. Right," Stephanie's story is proof that God is a good Father who gives good gifts to his children. In her book, Stephanie tells honest and humorous dating stories from her single days and the lessons she learned. An encouraging and thought-provoking read for anyone navigating singleness and dating.

PERRY NOBLE

Senior pastor of NewSpring Church and author of *Unleash!* and *Overwhelmed*

This book has a piece of my heart, and Stephanie now feels like a dear friend who knows my Starbucks order and shows up at my front door in her pajama-pants just to talk because she knows I've had a rough day. I laugh-cried through every inch of this book and felt every feeling right along with Stephanie. She has such a gift of bringing each "date" off the page and into full, living color for me to hold and learn from. I adore her vulnerability. And as I leaned into every story, I was once again reminded of the beauty found in life when we allow our relationships to teach us something deeper about ourselves and how we love.

KASEY VAN NORMAN
Bestselling author of *Named by God* and *Raw Faith*

Wise, warm, funny, and deep—Stephanie Rische writes in a way that will draw you in and keep you reading. Honest about the ache of being single when you long to be married, she has written a story that will deepen your hope and delight your heart. I loved traveling with Stephanie on her journey from one harrowing blind date to another, with loads of surprising experiences along the way.

ANN SPANGLER
Author of *Wicked Women of the Bible*

Bad dates, confusion in faith, real sin, fumbling around for grace: It takes guts to lay bare stories like these. It takes wit and charm to do it in a way that reads so endearingly. This book is a delightful telling of how God, in his kindness, allows himself to be seen.

LISA VELTHOUSE
Author of *Craving Grace* and coauthor of the *New York Times* bestseller *Your Beautiful Heart*

I WAS
BLIND
(Dating),
BUT NOW
I SEE

*my misadventures in dating,
waiting, and stumbling into love*

Stephanie Rische

**TYNDALE®
MOMENTUM**

*An Imprint of
Tyndale House Publishers, Inc.*

Visit Tyndale online at www.tyndale.com.

Visit Tyndale Momentum online at www.tyndalemomentum.com.

Visit www.stephanierische.com.

Tyndale Momentum and the Tyndale Momentum logo are registered trademarks of Tyndale House Publishers, Inc. Tyndale Momentum is an imprint of Tyndale House Publishers, Inc., Carol Stream, Illinois.

Library of Congress Cataloging-in-Publication Data
Rische, Stephanie.
    I was blind (dating), but now I see : my misadventures in dating, waiting, and stumbling into love / Stephanie Rische.
        pages cm
    Includes bibliographical references.
        ISBN 978-1-4964-0481-7 (sc)
1. Single people—Religious life. 2. Single people—Conduct of life. 3. Dating (Social customs)—Religious aspects—Christianity. 4. Marriage—Religious aspects—Christianity. I. Title.
    BV4596.S5R57 2016
    248.8'432--dc23   2015030322

Printed in the United States of America

22   21   20   19   18   17   16
7   6   5   4   3   2   1

For Daniel, my last blind date ever

Contents

Part 8: Journey

Author's Note

THIS BOOK IS NOT PRIMARILY A HISTORY, but rather a story, and as such, some of the timelines have been condensed or tweaked. This is fortunate for you, because it means you'll be spared from the really long, tedious stretches of my life when nothing interesting happened and I just did laundry and ate cereal and nearly missed my turns for work because I was so engrossed in whatever audiobook I was listening to.

Some names on the following pages have been changed. For example, I actually have four friends named Sarah, but I've reduced the number of Sarahs from four to one since I was concerned you'd need their Social Security numbers to keep them all straight. (Mom, I should mention that you're still Mom in this book, because there really just aren't many good pseudonyms for Mom.)

I also changed a few details to protect the privacy of my blind dates, although I have done so with a mixed conscience, because in a few instances, these guys should not be at large on the dating field. Please date at your own discretion.

Foreword

IS IT JUST ME OR DOES THE TERM *BLIND DATE* make you want to curl up in the fetal position due to post-traumatic stress? Anyone who has ever experienced that particular brand of awkwardness won't soon forget it. And if any subject is worthy of a book, this is it. Especially when most blind dates are set up by well-meaning married people who happen to know two single people and decide they should be totally compatible simply because they're both single. What could possibly go wrong?

But as I read this book, I realized Stephanie Rische has given us so much more than just a tale of looking for Mr. Right in a world of Mr. You Are So Wrong. It's a different kind of love story . . . a story about a God who pursues us, challenges us, and lets us wait on what we want most in life because he knows that the journey with him will ultimately teach us so much more than the destination.

So even if you are way past your dating years, there is a message for you within these pages about being faithful, staying true to who you are, and not waiting for that "big thing" before you live your life. Stephanie tells her story in eight sections: Waiting, Faithfulness, Community, Hope, Prayer, Gratitude, Joy, and Journey. These categories describe our life experience no matter where we are, where we've been, or where we're going. Each one is so crucial to the journey.

Stephanie shows us her longing for a husband; her fear of being left behind by her married friends; her disappointment in God during the waiting; her sense of being alone in the big, scary world; and the joy and gratitude that she found along the way. Because she writes with such tenderness, humor, and honesty, I found myself laughing out loud while reading one page and wiping away the tears running down my cheeks the next. I consider myself a funny snob, so I have deep, abiding love for anyone like Stephanie who can make me laugh out loud. (I'm like Cuba Gooding Jr. in *Jerry Maguire*, except my line is SHOW ME THE FUNNY.)

The characters Stephanie encounters as she goes on eight different blind dates in her quest to find a husband ring (no pun intended) so true to all those people and things we think look good on paper but turn out to be not quite what we wanted. *I Was Blind (Dating), but Now I See* is about a God who knows us so much better than we know ourselves, who pursues us and challenges us in ways we never could have imagined because He is a good Father. He wants to see us become who He created us to be and not just give us what we think looks best.

I'm excited that you have picked up this book and are about to go on this ride with Stephanie. Whether you are still in the world of blind dates or have finally met your match, you are in for a delightful experience.

Stephanie is that honest, funny, wise friend we all hope to have as we go through life. So grab a cup of coffee (or a Diet Coke), curl up, and prepare to laugh, to cry, and to see glimpses of your own life embedded in these words. You will walk away grateful for the experience and even more in love with our God.

Melanie Shankle
New York Times bestselling author of
Nobody's Cuter than You

Stumbling Blindly toward Grace

Break us with Thy grace.
DONALD BARNHOUSE

SOME PEOPLE COME UPON GRACE rather, well, gracefully. They seem to glide through life with wit and charm and perfect hair, and you get the sense that even if they have skeletons in their closets, they're filed away alphabetically in Rubbermaid totes.

I'm not one of those people.

I tend to be oblivious to grace until I stumble headlong into it. It's only when I'm on the ground, groping blindly in the darkness, that I recognize the unexpected beauty amid the brokenness. And as much as I'm smarting over the fall, I owe something to the pain and the downright clumsiness that brought me there in the first place.

I spent years on a quest for one thing, but God, in his circuitous grace, derailed me and brought me on an altogether different journey than the one I was expecting. And it was precisely during those moments when I was stumbling about that I began to recognize the grace all around, if only I would open my eyes to see it.

This is the story of how I tried really hard to find someone to fall in love with and get him to fall in love with me back—but how I mostly just ended up falling flat on my face. It's also the story of the unexpected ways God showed up when I finally admitted I couldn't pull myself up on my own.

I had my first lasting crush on a boy named Kevin when I was in fourth grade. With his floppy auburn hair, crooked grin, and pegged jeans, he was an '80s heartthrob. I, however, was quiet and unsure of myself, with a gap-toothed smile and corduroy pants that didn't quite hit the cool threshold. I never actually talked to Kevin, of course, but I was convinced that if he got to know me, he would surely like me back. That is, until the slumber party at Jasmine's house.

We were playing one of those slumber party games unique to ten-year-old girls wired on too much Mountain Dew, too little sleep, and scant parental supervision. The idea was to pass around a vase with a fake rose in it, and whenever it was your turn to hold the flower, you had to tell the other girls whom you had a crush on. When I was up, I shyly admitted I liked Kevin and then ducked my head, feeling the pink creep from my neck all the way up to my eyebrows.

Almost as soon as the words crossed my lips, one of the girls exclaimed, "Kevin? He would never like *you!*"

"Yeah," another girl chimed in. "He likes Stacey. She's cute."

I passed the vase to the next girl, desperately hoping I could blink back the tears before anyone noticed.

As elementary school marched into middle school and high school, things didn't change much for me in the boy department. I was still quiet and a few Esprit shirts shy of being popular. I didn't go to the homecoming dances, and no one asked me to prom. I tried to make the best of it my senior year by throwing a "non-prom" party for everyone else I knew who wasn't going, but truth be told, I wished a boy would notice me, think I was special, choose me. And although my little group of friends ended up having fun at our own party, the occasion wasn't exactly worthy of renting a limo for.

I went to a Christian college, where I was surrounded by a number of eligible, like-minded (and attractive) guys. But somehow I still felt invisible, and with the exception of one short-lived summer romance, I managed to get through all four years without being asked out on a single date. After I graduated and started navigating my twenties, I reached some significant milestones, like getting a job that morphed its way into a career and moving out of my rental unit into a place of my own. But as my friends and siblings started getting married, one summer after another, I still found myself decidedly alone.

I couldn't help but wonder if there was something broken in me that was apparently keeping all the men at bay. Was I not pretty enough? Not fun enough? Not engaging enough? Not dateable enough (whatever that meant)? And at another level, I wondered what to make of God's role in all of this. I longed for someone to do life with, someone to serve with, someone to love and to cherish—and someone who would love and cherish me back. Those seemed like good things—God things, even. I couldn't figure out why he was being so quiet about something that was so close to my heart. And so I started praying in earnest for God to bring the right man into my life.

Instead, he brought me matchmakers. Eight of them, to be precise.

So this is how a girl with practically zero dating experience and a shyness around boys that dated back to circa 1987 mustered up the courage to say yes to not one but eight blind dates over the course of five years. And how she did so with all the elegance of a pit bull in a tutu. But perhaps most of all, how God revealed so much of his amazing grace to her along the way that it left her lovestruck.

And although my story and my blind date adventures may be different from yours, my hope is that as you walk with me through these pages, you too will catch a glimpse of the one whose grace is enough to catch you when you stumble and whose love is deeper than you can fathom.

PART I

Waiting

When I'm in the cellar of affliction,
I look for the Lord's choicest wines.

SAMUEL RUTHERFORD

Blond Date

"HAVE FUN ON YOUR BLOND DATE," Nhu told me as she headed out the door.

Clearly there had been a communication breakdown somewhere along the way.

Nhu had been an even giddier version of her usual eighth-grade self when she found out about my date scheduled for the next day. I'd met Nhu at the church youth group, where I mentored her and a handful of other junior high girls. That day she'd come over to work on an essay for her English class since she and her mom didn't have a computer and she was still catching on to the nuances of the English language.

But once she got wind of my "blond date"—and when she discovered it was my first one, at that—all thoughts of homework quickly vaporized. She started peppering me with questions and offering advice about everything dating related—where we should go, what I should wear, and what she predicted this guy would look like (beyond the obvious blond hair).

We eventually got the definition worked out—that this guy was not necessarily blond, nor blind, for that matter. And then, to my surprise, Nhu blurted out, "What do *you* hope he's like?" She said it like it was the first time it had occurred to her that I might get some say in the matter. I suppose that's how you roll when you're thirteen.

I seized the teachable moment, telling her what was important to me when it came to someone I'd want to date. I was looking for a man with integrity, I said. Someone who loved God and did the right thing, even when it hurt. Someone who was serious enough to work hard but could also laugh himself silly. A man who would honor me and love me at my best and my worst.

At some point I looked over at Nhu and realized her eyes were glazing over. Sure enough, I'd surpassed the thirty-second teenager-accessibility window.

"One more thing," I added. "I guess I always pictured myself with a brown-haired guy."

As it turned out, Blond Date did, indeed, have blond streaks in his hair. Unfortunately, that was where the highlights ended. So to speak.

I arrived at Jamba Juice a few minutes early, so I wasn't surprised Blond Date hadn't arrived yet. Truth be told, I was a bit relieved, as it would buy me time to dry my sweaty palms and figure out what drink I should order to convey that I was neither a glutton nor a calorie counter. Perfectly natural, of course.

Five minutes ticked by. I had my order down by now. Ten minutes. I was eyeing every male who approached the door, alternately hoping it would be him and praying it wouldn't, based on whether his car looked like a candidate for the scrap metal yard, whether his shoes clashed with his pants, and other such deep inner qualities.

Fifteen minutes. The girl behind the counter was now giving me pitying looks. Twenty minutes. I wished I'd done more research on blind-date etiquette. *How long do you wait before conceding you've been stood up?*

And another thing: What role did the matchmaker play once the ball had gotten rolling? I'd feel like the worst kind of snitch to call her with a report about my date's AWOL status, and I couldn't think of a way to pull off a casual check-in, where I'd nonchalantly fish for hints as to whether he'd lost interest somewhere between Tuesday and the nearest Jamba Juice.

The truth was, I didn't even know Debbie, the matchmaker, all that well. My brother and sister had played sports with her kids in high school, so we often found ourselves cheering together on the bleachers at basketball and softball games. Several years had passed since then, but Debbie thought of me one day when she was talking to her friend (Blond Date's mom), who was fretting over her son's bachelordom. As they were lamenting over how "all he needed was to meet a nice girl," my name popped into Debbie's mind.

I'm not entirely sure why I agreed to the setup, since for me, even answering a call from an unknown number felt like an act of daredevil-esque courage. I'd always assumed blind dates fell into the category of Things I Just Don't Do, right up there with cliff diving and juggling knives. I wasn't sure I could sit and make small talk with a stranger for an hour, let alone do said scary activity with a *date*. As I tried to figure out how to respond to her voice mail, I thought through the booby traps of saying yes: (1) I'd have to navigate the tricky, alien world of dating, with its unwritten codes and expectations; (2) in a short window of time, I'd have to try to represent myself accurately yet winsomely enough that this person would go out of his way to see me again; and (3) I'd have to try to eat something while looking cute and preferably not getting anything stuck between my teeth.

All the tallies seemed to be lining up in the "con" column, but there was one potential pro that had the power to outweigh them all:

the *what-if*. This probably wouldn't go anywhere . . . but *what if* it did? This guy probably wasn't my soul mate . . . but *what if* he was?

There was something else I had going for me: I never bumped into Debbie in the course of normal life. So if things blew up or fizzled out, I'd be able to wallow in anonymity.

Of course, I hadn't counted on Blond Date not showing up at all. Twenty-five minutes. By now I was moving from twinges of disappointment to bouts of indignation. But each time I got angry, I'd picture him in a fiery crash somewhere between his house and Jamba Juice and cut him some slack. I decided to give him thirty minutes, and after that I was out of there.

As my eyes flicked compulsively between the parking lot and my watch, I heard a voice behind me. "Excuse me," the girl behind the counter said. "Are you waiting for someone?" So much for my play-it-cool strategy.

I nodded lamely.

"Well, he just called and said to tell you he's running late."

Forty-three minutes after the prearranged time, Blond Date showed up.

"Did you get the message I'd be late?" he asked. "I was in the middle of a really intense game of soccer."

Soccer? Not a fiery car crash? I took a breath, determined to give him the benefit of the doubt.

"Oh," I said. "Do you play on a team?"

"No, it's just a bunch of guys who play pickup in the park near my house."

At least I was getting a Banana Berry Smoothie with a boost of vitamin C for my efforts. And he *had* showered, so that showed some effort, if not time-management skills.

As soon as we ordered (to his credit, he paid), it was time to face the dilemma I'd had plenty of time to ponder since arriving. The thing is, this particular Jamba Juice had no seating. And it was a brisk November day in blustery Chicagoland.

I'd scoped out our options and figured our best bet was to sit on a bench just outside the building. I pitched the idea to Blond Date as we walked out of the place, but he countered with the suggestion that we chat in my car instead.

"In my car?" Something about having this person I'd never met (and someone I'd spent the past forty-three minutes being peeved at) in my vehicle felt awkward at best. Maybe even a little creepy.

But he was persistent. "It's too cold out here."

I resisted the urge to say something about it not being too cold for pickup soccer.

And so it was that we ended up sitting in my car and making awkward small talk while drinking our smoothies.

"So, tell me about yourself," he said.

I swallowed, willing myself not to feel like I was at a job interview.

But it was a fair question. We had covered the subjects we knew we had in common (i.e., our matchmaker) in the span of about thirty seconds. When you go on a normal date, you theoretically already have some common ground to start from. But we were starting from scratch. How could it *not* feel like an interview?

Please don't ask what three adjectives I'd use to describe myself!

I lobbed some questions to Blond Date about soccer, but my knowledge of the game was limited to fourth-grade gym class and how I thought Mia Hamm had a cool name, so that didn't go very far.

Our humor styles were in different orbits too. Despite my best attempts to make him laugh, he remained stoic. *Does it only make things worse if I explain that was a joke? Or should I just move on?*

I decided it was better to abort and reroute the conversation.

"I'm hosting a birthday party for my friend next weekend," I said. "I'm thinking of having fondue."

And *that's* when he laughed.

Wait—that wasn't the joke! We passed the joke exit several mile markers ago! I hoped my face didn't betray my indignation.

"I didn't know anyone did that anymore," he said by way of explanation.

Eventually Blond Date looked at his watch. "Well, it's been an hour," he said, "which is my rule for first dates." He reached out his hand for an inelegant side-by-side handshake.

"It was nice meeting you," he said. And that was that.

Well. I'd always pictured myself with a brown-haired guy anyway.

In the Waiting Room

❀

I WAS SITTING in the waiting room at the health clinic, anticipating a shot in each arm for my upcoming trip overseas. As I sat there surrounded by fussy toddlers, I was just a little bit jealous of the tikes. I was feeling pretty whiny myself, but I figured now that I was in my twenties, I had probably passed the window for socially acceptable public whining.

I tried to distract myself by alternately eavesdropping on other people's conversations and trying to read the "Don't blame us if this shot is a terrible mistake" brochure. Surprisingly enough, neither activity did much to settle my agitation. So I sat there in the waiting room, just thinking about waiting. I started to wonder if one of the worst parts of the whole waiting game is how alone it makes you feel. Even in a room full of other waiters.

The truth was, it wasn't just the line in the health clinic that had my nerves frayed. My mind was on my closet at home, where

I'd just hung my fourth bridesmaid dress. Without warning, the waiting-for-a-husband ache launched itself from its generally contained place in my gut to somewhere near my esophagus. I'd like to say that the words that formed inside me in that moment were a prayer, but I'm pretty sure they sounded to God's ears exactly like what they were: a whine. *When will it be my turn to hang a white dress in my closet?*

I'd never been one of those girls with dreams of a fairy princess wedding. I hadn't thought much about bridesmaid dress palettes, what china pattern I'd register for, what little favors I'd put by the place settings at the reception, or the benefits of strapless dresses vs. those with cap sleeves. But for as long as I could remember, I'd wanted what came with the wedding package: the man who'd always be in my corner, the father of my future children, the steady permanence of "till death do us part." I guess I just assumed the process of meeting Mr. Right would be pretty straightforward. And I figured somewhere in my midtwenties would be about the right time for that to happen. I may have even told God as much on an occasion or two.

After college, I watched as things came together rather effortlessly for my friends. They'd meet a guy—at work, at church, at a party—and it wasn't long before they were hanging out, then dating seriously, then engaged, and before I knew it, my friends were joining the ranks of *Mrs.* But for whatever reason, nothing seemed to be working out for me. There certainly weren't guys lining up at my door, and when I did meet someone, it seemed like there was more fizzle than sizzle. Would my turn ever come?

How much longer, God?

It was something I'd asked before. But for the first time, sitting on that sticky, plastic waiting-room chair, a horrifying follow-up question barged in, unbidden. *Is the waiting my fault somehow?*

Was I stuck while everyone else was moving on because I was doing something wrong? And perhaps more to the point, was something wrong with *me*?

Just then I was called back into a rather stark room with a green curtain for a door. An all-business nurse with a gruff voice jabbed a needle in my arm before I could even ask her if it would hurt.

∞

When I got home, I found myself still feeling a bit sore, and I was pretty sure it wasn't just my tender bicep. I decided it was time to nail God down. Was my waiting some kind of punishment, a spiritual time-out of sorts?

I stewed for a while, trying to distract myself by getting a snack, checking my phone, turning on a movie, and checking my phone again. The one place with answers was, as usual, my last resort.

As I searched through the Bible, I was shocked to discover I was in good company. In fact, the more I looked, the more hard-pressed I became to find anyone God used in big ways who wasn't at some point refined in the waiting room.

There was Joseph, who surely wondered at times whether he'd rot in prison before his dreams became a reality. And Hannah, who prayed and agonized for a child, each month a stinging reminder that she was—again—not pregnant. There was Moses, who wandered around the wilderness (sans GPS) for forty years, awaiting the Promised Land; Abraham and Sarah, who waited until well past menopause for their promised son; David, who hung out in caves with a crazy king on his tail, wondering when he'd receive his promised crown. And that's to say nothing of generation after generation of God followers who longed for the promised Messiah.

Then one morning I unearthed a story about waiting from an event I wouldn't have expected: the raising of Lazarus. In the past I'd read John 11 solely as Lazarus's story. But this time I found myself looking at things through his sisters' eyes.

Jesus was good friends with Martha, Mary, and Lazarus, and Scripture says he crashed at their place fairly regularly. So surely when he got word that Lazarus was sick, he'd rush to Bethany and heal him . . . right? But then I hit this haunting sentence: "Although Jesus loved Martha, Mary, and Lazarus, he stayed where he was for the next two days" (John 11:5-6). Even though I knew the story had a happy ending, I found myself compelled to shout, "Hello! What were you waiting for, Jesus? That's not love!"

Martha and Mary were slightly more diplomatic, but their sentiment was the same: "Lord, if only you had been here . . ." (verses 21, 32).

According to Jesus, the death of Lazarus "happened for the glory of God" (verse 4). Granted, the healing of Lazarus would have been remarkable and glory-worthy all on its own. But Jesus had a bigger plan that couldn't have been accomplished if Lazarus hadn't spent some time in the grave, if his sisters hadn't spent some time in the waiting room themselves. Miracles, it turns out, don't always come in expedient packages. Pierre Teilhard de Chardin, a philosopher and Jesuit priest, put it this way: "Above all, trust in the slow work of God."

There's a soul-level kind of intimacy that takes place in the midst of waiting, if only we're willing to crack open the door of our hearts enough to let it in. I wonder if Mary and Martha almost missed Jesus' act of vulnerability and compassion, as it fell somewhere between their intense grief and one of Jesus' most astounding miracles. I almost missed it too—just a short verse tucked between the drama of the other events: "Then Jesus wept" (verse 35). I have to admit that this show of emotion struck me as a bit odd at first. Jesus knew he would raise Lazarus from the dead in just a few moments. Yet he still wept?

I read one commentary that attempted a philosophical explanation of Jesus' tears—that he was weeping for the fallen state of humanity or for the paltry faith of his followers. I'm no theologian, but I opted for a more basic interpretation. He hurt because he saw Mary and Martha's pain. His heart broke to see their hearts breaking.

He didn't insist that they get over their waiting ache; he walked through it with them.

Did I believe he'd do the same for me? Did I believe that in my own waiting room, I was never really alone? That the flesh-and-blood God who shed real saltwater tears was with me? I wanted to sit with Mary and Martha in the waiting and realize that sometimes God doesn't give us what we ask for—sometimes he gives us something better. Himself. In between the heartache and the miracle, right smack-dab in the middle of the waiting, he weeps with us. And for now, that was enough.

Even if I met my husband-to-be the next day, I knew I'd still be waiting for something. Or rather, for some*one*. No human being, after all, could fill the God-sized longing that he had planted inside of me—that he places inside every one of us.

That didn't take the ache away, but putting words to it felt like a start. And maybe I'd leave some extra room in my closet for a white dress. Just in case.

Tokens of His Love

I'D BEEN IN Grandma and Grandpa's basement countless times over the years. But until that blistering summer afternoon, each visit had been quite ordinary. Filled with fond memories, but ordinary nonetheless.

Grandma and Grandpa's basement was the place we kids would go when the grown-ups got too long-winded with their reminiscences, when my dad and his siblings were starting in on yet another when-I-was-your-age story. We'd catch Mom's eye for permission to escape to our basement hideout, where we'd make our customary pilgrimage to the family photo wall, plastered with pictures of my dad and his eleven siblings and a whole slew of our cousins, all the while oblivious to the family intrigue that beckoned from just behind the closet door.

It had been a while since I'd been in Grandma and Grandpa's basement, and now this visit would likely be my last. After my grandfather's stroke, it was clear to everyone that the time had come for them to move into an assisted living facility.

Grandma put a positive spin on the transition. "It's a good chance to downsize, honey," she assured me. But I knew it couldn't be easy to close the door on so many memories.

When I arrived that morning, I quickly discovered that Grandma was in auctioneer mode, and the goal was to send me home with as many treasures as possible. So armed with several large black plastic bags, we scoured each room of the house together, stuffing the bags with more blankets, kitchen gadgets, and embroidered tablecloths than my little condo would be able to hold.

By the time we got to the basement, my decision-making capabilities, not to mention my plastic bags, were overloaded. Surely there could be no surprises left. (What could top the discovery of twenty-one unopened Kleenex boxes in the upstairs closet?) I was starting to check out a bit, doing some mental Tetris to determine if everything would fit in my car, when Grandma opened the basement closet and came across a large garment bag near the back. As she tugged the zipper, I heard her breath lodge in her throat.

Finally the bag opened enough for me to get a glimpse inside. And there, as if he'd just stepped out of them, were my grandfather's army jackets. A short flight jacket. A formal coat with stars on the lapel. A khaki lieutenant's coat. A long overcoat. I glanced over at Grandma and watched her green eyes fill with tears. "I'm so proud of him," she whispered.

I stood spellbound as Grandma began her tale of the two agonizing years she'd waited for Grandpa to return from World War II. They'd met in the hiking club at college (Grandma confessed that she'd joined just so she could get to know the tall, dashing fellow freshman). They soon became sweethearts, dreaming together and making plans for the future. But then Grandpa left halfway through college to fly bomber planes with the Eighth Air Force.

"We were promised to each other," she told me. "We knew we

wanted to get married, but Grandpa didn't have the money for a ring yet." She swallowed, and I saw that her eyes were shining. "So many of his friends got married before they went off to war, but he didn't want to make things harder for me in case he never came back.

"Oh, look! There's something else!" She grabbed my hand, and we were instantly transported back sixty-plus years. Rummaging behind a stack of boxes, we uncovered a faded metal trunk with my grandfather's name stenciled evenly on the side. We wrestled the rusty hinges loose, and after releasing a whiff of dust and aged paper, it finally creaked open. Time was suspended for a moment as we gazed, mesmerized, at the contents of the trunk.

"Letters," I finally whispered.

Letters, indeed—the entire trunk was full of them. On one side were bundles of blue envelopes, tied together with dainty white ribbons and addressed in Grandma's looping script.

"I wrote him every night," she said.

On the other side of the trunk, in a hodgepodge of smudged, tattered envelopes, were letters from her lieutenant serving across the ocean.

"In those days I worked at the college library to pay my tuition," Grandma told me. "Every day on my lunch break, I'd change out of my heels and make the fifteen-minute run through the hills of downtown Seattle to my apartment . . . just to see if there was a letter from your grandfather." She'd barely have time to snatch a sandwich before heading back to work on the nickel streetcar, if she had the money.

"Has anyone else read these?" I asked.

"Oh no, honey." She gave a shy laugh. "Not till after I'm dead."

We latched the trunk, and Grandma was back in the basement again, mindful of the dust covering the palms of her hands. Until Grandpa's recent hospital stay, she hadn't been apart from him for some sixty years. After he had returned from the war, they got married as soon as the church was available (a Tuesday morning, in fact), and ever since, Grandma had been by his side.

"How did you do it, Grandma?" I asked. "How could you handle the waiting . . . the not knowing?"

"I didn't really have a choice," she said simply.

This petite woman in front of me, sweet as she was, was made of some tough fabric.

In one sense she was right—she didn't have a choice about whether she'd wait. She had no control over when the war would be over, no sway over whether her fiancé would have to go on yet another mission, no guarantee that he'd return in one piece. But there was one thing she did have a choice about: *how* she'd wait.

So each day she did the only thing she could: She sat down with her blue stationery and wrote letters to the one she loved. She let the waiting make her stronger, more faithful, more dependent on the God she believed was bigger than this war. She didn't waste the waiting. She allowed it to make her better.

As Grandma and Grandpa's place faded in my rearview mirror for the last time, I realized that I, too, had a choice. Would I continue my treadmill routine of moping around and wishing for a man with husband potential to materialize? Or I would I attempt waiting Grandma-style—running to the mailbox each day, full of hope and anticipation that God would show himself to me, whether that came in the form I was expecting or not?

I hoped that at the end of this waiting—however it would end—I would be stronger somehow. More ready for the God I was ultimately waiting for.

More like Grandma.

Spiritual Breath Holding

It was Advent, one of my favorite seasons. The mere word had the power to conjure up nostalgic images from my childhood: the musty attic smell as I helped Mom pull the wreath from its yearlong hibernation. The anticipation of finally being old enough to light one of the four candles by myself at the dinner table. Sitting beside the crackling fire in my pajamas each evening and opening one of the twenty-five little windows on the Advent calendar.

But this year I just wasn't feeling it. It would have been fine by me if everyone agreed to turn the calendar and skip right from November to January. If I had to hear one more engagement ring commercial touting, "He went to Jared!" heaven help me, I was going to go on a monthlong boycott of every form of media. Christmas music notwithstanding.

I drove to church on the first Sunday in December, half anticipating and half dreading the sweet tradition of having families with young children light the Advent candles at the front of the church. I loved seeing the little girls in their fancy dresses, hair in silky bows for the occasion, and the boys looking squirmy and ready to bolt right out of their button-up shirts. But this Christmas it seemed like one more aching reminder that another year had passed, and once again, I was sitting in the pew by myself, with nary a bow-headed child on the horizon.

I braced myself for a feel-good sermon about anticipating Christmas, grateful for the dim lighting and hoping it would provide cover in the event that my tear ducts betrayed me.

I was surprised when the pastor set about painting a grittier picture of Advent than I'd expected. Historically, he said, it wasn't so warm and fuzzy. It's easy to forget that during the first Advent, the faithful who were waiting for the Messiah had access to mere shadow-glimpses of what—and who—was to come.

With the benefit of hindsight, we can now look back and realize that *of course* Jesus came at just the right time—taking his place among the shepherds, the angels, and the barn animals at the manger. But those men and women who lived before his birth didn't have our advantage of retrospect. Sure, they'd heard the prophecies about Bethlehem, the whispered hints from Isaiah and Micah and the rest. But they had no Nativity scene template, no illustrated calendar counting down the days until December 25. Instead, they faced several hundred agonizing years of silence between the last official word from the Lord and the arrival of the Messiah.

I wondered if they felt the ache—that beautiful longing for something—all the while knowing it wasn't a reality yet. As much as I wanted to experience the thrill of the arrival, to celebrate the sweet taste of a miracle fulfilled, I had to admit there was a certain quiet beauty to the waiting season that preceded it.

In retrospect, I suppose the Grinchy Christmas had started back in October, when I got the call from my little sister. She's not typically one for phone chatting, so I knew something was up. But it was taking her a while to spit it out.

Finally she said, "You know . . . Ted and I have been dating for a while now." *Yeah. I know.* "Well, we were thinking about spending Thanksgiving at Mom and Dad's . . ." *Okay* . . . "And, well, we were thinking about Christmas . . ." It suddenly hit me with all the grace of a charging rhino.

"Christmas," I said. "You want to spend Christmas with Ted's family." I swallowed twice. Why hadn't I seen this coming?

Ever since my younger brother had started dating Amber, he'd been on the every-other-Christmas plan, meaning he alternated holidays between our family and her family. It was all quite logical, really, but that didn't stop me from wishing on the off years that my sister-in-law had come from a Jewish family. I'd happily give them Hanukkah every year in exchange for Christmas. But with no such luck, my little brother would be spending Christmas in St. Louis this year.

And now my baby sister would be gone too.

"You should go," I finally heard myself say. I was even more surprised than Meghan when my voice came out sounding so calm—supportive, even. And the truth was, at a fundamental level, I couldn't help but be supportive. Ted was the only guy Meghan had brought home thus far who had been worthy of the sisterly stamp of approval.

When Meghan was in first grade, she started consistently beating my brother and me at the-card-game-that-shall-never-be-spoken-aloud-again—a game based on skill and speed. Kyle was in middle school and I was in high school at the time, and it was rather demoralizing to be trumped by a kid whose diapers we'd been changing just a few years ago. After one particularly painful defeat, my brother and I packed up the game and announced we'd never play it again. After Meghan went crying to Mom, I remember making this declaration to my brother: "When she starts dating, she's going to have trouble meeting her match."

I should have known she and Ted were meant to be before they even became an item. They were on the college track team together, and at the NCAA national championship her senior year, they were winning simultaneous national championships—Meghan at pole vault, and Ted at high jump on the other side of the track.

Ted was, in every way, her match—intellectually, athletically, spiritually. He was strong enough not to get bulldozed by her fierce determination, but he also had an easygoing-enough temperament and a sense of humor to balance her out. And he could even beat her at cards on occasion.

So I was happy for her, and it made sense for her to spend Christmas with Ted and his family. But I was sad for myself, the spinster sister. As the oldest of my siblings, I was used to being first at things, not last. I was used to doing the leaving, not being left.

Somehow I managed to utter a cheerful good-bye before doing one of those slow-motion slumps against the wall in the hallway— you know, the kind where the guy in the action movie gets stabbed in the gut and falls dramatically to the floor, hand clutching his side. Only in my case, there wasn't blood, just melodrama.

"All I want for Christmas is my two siblings," I sang in a lame parody of a Christmas song that's lame enough all on its own. Nobody laughed.

I spent most of the shopping days till Christmas being generally grumpy about my newfound only-child status. And each week as Christmas neared, it seemed like I was accosted with yet another validation of my hypothesis that not only was the holiday season intended to guilt you into spending ridiculous sums of money on people you've been neglecting for the better part of the year; it's also a brazen attempt to make lonely people all the lonelier.

Case in point: the dreaded work Christmas party, where everyone else brought their spouse/significant other, and I showed up alone. Again. While they paired off two by two, like so many animals on Noah's ark, I sat there concentrating intently on my beverage, trying to convince myself that this was a better alternative than watching a movie at home in my pj's.

I did get a free dinner, I conceded. And frankly, the conversation with my friend Dorothy alone would have been worth the price of admission. At seventy, she was among the retirees who had been invited, and unlike me, she didn't seem to have conflicted feelings about coming alone to this gathering. In fact, I was pretty sure I'd never seen her so downright giddy before.

"I never drink caffeine," she confided to me. "But this is such a special occasion. I just let myself go and had some decaf coffee!"

I guessed I could learn a thing or two from Dorothy about what constitutes a "special occasion." If only I could get that much joy out of a cup of decaf.

Still, at the end of the evening, when all the male guests went out into the cold, snowy darkness to pull up cars for their dates, I wished for the umpteenth time that season that I wasn't alone. I bundled my coat around me and trudged through the parking lot in my heels, promising myself that next year would be different. I'd bring a boy, I declared to myself. Or at the very least, some boots.

Before I knew it, Christmas was several days away. In the midst of my own moping about the fact that our family traditions wouldn't be the same this year and that everyone was moving on without me, I'm ashamed to say it never occurred to me that it would be a tough holiday for my parents, too.

Mom and I tried to make plans for our usual Christmas traditions, but Dad was even more resistant to making plans than usual. We just couldn't get him to commit to anything—which church service we'd go to, what we'd have for Christmas dinner, when we'd go on our annual holiday moonlight walk.

In the meantime, I talked to a friend who had lost a child in the past year.

"This will be our first Christmas without our son," she told me. "So we decided to do the most opposite thing we could think of this year." Instead of staying home in snowy Michigan, they were heading to Florida.

"I just couldn't bear the thought that there would be an empty chair at Christmas breakfast, that there would be one less stocking to fill, that our family photo in front of the tree would be missing a face," she said. "I'm sure we'll go back to our old traditions someday, but it's just too raw right now. At least the beach will be a change of scenery."

After our conversation I sat glued to my chair, trying to imagine what it would be like to deal with such a gaping hole. A *permanent* hole. And also feeling selfish and pathetic for thinking I had anything at all to complain about this Christmas.

I called my dad. "What do *you* want to do this Christmas?" In all these weeks of fussing and making plans, how had it never occurred to me to solicit his input? I promised myself I'd be ready for whatever he had in mind. (And maybe a tiny part of me was thinking, *Daytona Beach, here we come!*)

He barely hesitated. It was like he'd been prepping for this question for months. "I've been wanting to help you redo the kitchen floor in your condo," he said.

"Thanks, Dad. That would be great. But I mean what do you want to do for *Christmas*?"

Sure enough, though, that's exactly what he meant. And so it was that we made a trip to the store amid all the last-minute holiday shoppers to stock up on wood flooring, nails, floor glue, and a blade for the circular saw.

All day on Christmas Eve, the two of us went back and forth between my kitchen and the chilly garage, which constituted the makeshift workshop where we tried to wrestle each pesky wood piece into submission.

Nothing about the scene felt particularly Christmassy—not even our sound track for the day, which consisted of Dad's favorite Jimmy

Buffett album on constant repeat, along with a variety of choice words that flew out unsolicited each time the uncooperative wood panels splintered off at the wrong place, despite our careful work. Or, to be more precise, despite *Dad's* careful work. Because who am I kidding—I pretty much just held the boards while he sawed and handed him the tools I could identify (which was, for the most part, limited to the duct tape).

At the end of the evening, when Dad and I stood back and surveyed our work, we were sore but satisfied. No, it didn't feel like Christmas. But maybe that was as it should have been that year. At least until the rawness wore off a little.

One quiet evening near the close of the year, as I sat reading and drinking my second cup of hot chocolate for the evening and shooting the occasional admiring glance in the direction of my new floor, I came across these words by Frederick Buechner:

> In the silence of a midwinter dusk there is far off in the deeps
> of it somewhere a sound so faint that for all you can tell it
> may be the sound of the silence itself. You hold your breath to
> listen. . . . For a second you catch the whiff in the air of some
> fragrance that reminds you of a place you've never been and
> a time you have no words for. You are aware of the beating of
> your heart. The extraordinary thing that is about to happen
> is matched only by the extraordinary moment just before it
> happens. Advent is the name of that moment.[1]

Something about Buechner's metaphor clicked in my soul. Advent wasn't a pretty wreath or a glowing ring of candles. It was holding your breath.

There's nothing very sentimental about that. When I was a kid, we used to have breath-holding contests in my neighbor's pool, and the thing I remember most is that dizzying feeling when I came to the surface, sucking air and clinging to the ledge. It certainly wasn't nostalgic or pretty, but as that oxygen coursed through my lungs, I felt *alive*.

What must those God followers have felt like in that time between Malachi and Matthew? Did they wonder if God would ever speak to his people again? Would he make good on his promises? Would their Advent be worth it all in the end?

There's no way to know how many people kept holding their breath for the Messiah, but Scripture gives an account of one of the standouts: Simeon.

The Holy Spirit had revealed to Simeon that he would see the Messiah before he died. The Bible says he was old by the time Jesus came along, and I have to wonder: If I'd been in his sandals, would I have been ready? Or would I have gotten distracted and moved on to another cause, another goal by then? Or would I have had a twenty-year chip on my shoulder, bitter that God hadn't hurried up and fulfilled the plan already?

But the next phrase in Luke's account struck me: Simeon "was *eagerly* waiting for the Messiah to come and rescue Israel" (Luke 2:25, emphasis added). That's how I wanted my Advent to be. Eager. Not whiny. Not worried. Not impatient . . . but not getting so comfy here that I forget what I'm holding my breath for, either.

And in that moment, an epiphany of sorts came to me. Why not celebrate four weeks of Advent now? Sure, the calendar was all wrong and Christmas was already in the rearview mirror, but maybe I needed to declare a personal Advent—a few weeks of dedicating myself to waiting well, Simeon style.

So I packed up all my Christmas decorations . . . except my Advent wreath. After a little digging, I discovered that according to church tradition, the candle for each week has a symbolic meaning. The first one is for hope. The second, love. The candle for the third week—the lone pink one—stands for joy. And the last one is for peace. Each morning I'd get up before dawn and light a candle, asking God for one of those four gifts. I'd pray that my waiting wouldn't be stagnant, that it would instead be infused with hope, with love, with joy, with peace.

While everyone else was returning gifts and putting away their Christmas trees, I'd spend the next four weeks in the Temple with Simeon and Frederick Buechner. Just holding my breath.

PART 2

Faithfulness

Do not be upset if you do not immediately receive
what you asked God to give you.
The Lord wants to give you greater things
than you have even thought to pray for—
to teach you to persevere in prayer.

EVAGRIUS OF PONTUS

The Professor

DURING MY SENIOR YEAR at a small Christian college, I'd met all the requirements for my major and had room in my schedule for an extra elective. Feeling optimistic on the man front despite my practically nonexistent dating record, I decided to enroll in a class called Christian Marriage. Who knows—my future husband might have been right around the corner. And on the off chance that I met him in said class, wouldn't *that* make a great story to tell the kids one day? (Alas, as it turned out, the enrollment for Christian Marriage 101 was approximately 96 percent female.)

One of our early assignments for the class was to make a four-column list of the traits we'd want in a spouse: "Must-haves," "Would likes," "Would not likes," and "Deal breakers." With all the naive idealism of a twenty-one-year-old, I made a marriage potential checklist the length of Princess Di's wedding dress train. I had every little detail of Mr. Perfect pigeonholed, all the way down to eye color, worship style, and gardening habits.

So, several years later, when I got set up on a blind date with an actual college professor, I was ready. I knew exactly what I was looking for.

The Professor and I met for dinner on a rainy evening, halfway between where both of us lived—he came from downtown Chicago by train while I made my way from the suburbs in my little silver car, windshield wipers doing double-time. I sat in the car for a few moments before getting out, partly to get my umbrella ready and partly in an attempt to calm my racing pulse.

As I power walked into the restaurant, trying to protect as much of my meticulously flat-ironed hair as possible, I thought about what our matchmaker had told me about The Professor. I'd been set up by a coworker I really admired—someone smart and savvy and accomplished, someone I aspired to be like one day. I felt honored that she'd thought of me and gone out of her way to introduce me to someone. Still, I was trying to keep my hopes in check, seeing as how for all I knew, the guy might have incurable halitosis or the back hair of a woolly mammoth, but based on the information I had so far, he sounded like a dead ringer for my Marriage Material Checklist.

After an awkward half hug/half handshake, we found a table in a quietish corner of the café. As we started talking, I was overcome by two growing realizations. First, The Professor did, indeed, exhibit a startling number of the traits on The List. Places a high value on education? Check. Appreciates the finer points of grammar, like the fact that *irregardless* isn't really a word? Check. Has an affinity for literature, particularly novels by dead British guys? Check. Prefers autumn as his season of choice? Check. Enjoys a good cup of coffee? Check.

But at the same time I was coming to a second equally startling revelation: I hadn't been so bored since my seventy-year-old friend Dorothy gave me an extensive rundown on her latest gastroenterologist appointment. And as for The Professor, he looked like he'd rather be getting a root canal.

I remember reading a book once about how to be an effective conversationalist. The author used tennis as a metaphor: A question is like a serve, with the goal of launching a topic. Then both parties volley the topic back and forth. Only in this case, it felt like with each attempt at a return, the ball just flubbed into the net.

"So, what TV shows do you like?"

"Oh, I don't have a TV."

(Awkward pause.)

"What would you get your doctorate in?"

"Um, I'm not sure I'd want to get a doctorate."

(Sounds of chewing.)

After launching a few more conversational tennis balls, we finished our paninis and The Professor gave me a rather noncommittal send-off—something to the effect of, "Well, maybe we'll talk again sometime."

And I said something equally charming, like, "Yeah, okay."

About a week later The Professor and I went out again, with similar results: more check marks, more yearnings for root canals.

At a loss for what to make of all this, I talked to my friends Catherine and Art, who had been married for several years. I appreciated their knack for telling the truth but doing it in a way that went down like sugar chasing the proverbial medicine.

"What do you think?" I asked. "He's a nice guy, and he matches so many of my requirements. But I'm just not feeling it."

That's when Catherine cooked up a plan. We'd have a party and invite The Professor. That way I could see him in a different setting, and best of all, I could get my friends' take on him.

We decided to plan a "practice Thanksgiving" at my house, based on the premise that the best food of the year shouldn't be relegated to just one day. A group of about eight of us went to a park near my house, where we all played touch football (well, all except for The

Professor, who had apparently sustained an unfortunate injury to his foot the day before), tossing the ball back and forth enough times to justify the potluck feast awaiting us.

When we got back to my place, I went about setting the table while making casual chitchat with The Professor. My back was to the wall, and The Professor was facing me. Art was standing just behind The Professor, meaning I could see him, but The Professor couldn't.

When The Professor and I were in the midst of some unremarkable conversation, Art caught my eye with some dramatic arm flailing. He was mouthing *No!* while gesticulating wildly, hand to throat, in a clear cue to cut this guy off. I managed to keep my composure long enough to finish laying out the spoons before escaping to the privacy of my bathroom, where I could finally let out a strangled chortle.

After everyone else left, Catherine and Art stayed to help me clean up and do the dishes . . . and to have a little debriefing session.

"I feel kind of guilty," I said. "I mean, there's nothing *wrong* with him. . . . Shouldn't I have some quantifiable reason not to want to hang out with him?"

As Catherine listened, I ticked off The Professor's pros and cons, analyzing every trait, from his admirable vocabulary to his commendable church involvement to his hit-or-miss wardrobe selections.

Catherine paused from the stack of cups she was gathering from the table. "What about you, Stephanie?" she asked gently.

I gave her a look of sheer befuddlement.

"Think of all the things you would bring to a relationship."

What do I bring to a relationship? It had hardly occurred to me that I had a pro-con list myself. I suddenly found that all my concentration was required to load the silverware into the dishwasher.

Catherine, good friend that she was, went on to list the things she appreciated about me—the positive traits I would contribute to a relationship. Something washed over me in that moment—a sense of being known and accepted as I was. And there was something about being aware that I had a friend who would stay by my side after seeing both the good and the ugly that gave me the courage to take an honest look at myself.

Perhaps even more significant, her faithfulness felt like a reflection of the way God saw me. If my friend would stick by me faithfully, knowing what she was getting herself into, maybe I could dare to believe that God was in this for the long haul too. His blessings weren't conditional on whether my pros outweighed my cons—he was willing to accept the whole package.

After Catherine and Art left, I stayed up late, Catherine's question swirling in my head. I had spent so much time evaluating, analyzing, excavating, trying to figure out if this guy measured up to The List. But what about *me*? Did I have a clear idea of who I was—my own pros and cons? How could I know what I wanted in a guy if I didn't know myself first?

And so that night I grabbed my journal and tore out the page with The List on it. I shredded it into hundreds of pieces, confetti-style.

Then I turned to a fresh page and starting making a new list. The words flowed as quickly as my pen could scratch them down. It felt like a rare moment of clarity—like this awareness of being known and loved anyway allowed me to hold a mirror to myself without swinging to either extreme of self-degradation or false modesty and capture a snapshot of the real me—warts, beauty marks, and all.

Pro: Will stick by my people.
Con: Prone to martyr-like tendencies.
Pro: Determined to see something through to the end.
Con: Crumble when I consistently fall short of perfection.
Pro: Will fight for the underdog.
Con: Envious of the top dog.
Pro: Can whip up a mean pan of peanut butter brownies.
Con: Haven't swept the floor in a good four weeks.

This time my list wasn't about if another person measured up to some arbitrary set of standards. It was about who I was . . . and who I wanted to be.

It was about who I was becoming.

The Professor and I exchanged a few halfhearted e-mails after that, leaving us in that post-date limbo of not having reason enough to move forward but not having reason enough to cut things off. Eventually the e-mails tapered off and finally stopped. I owed him something, though—not for the panini, but for what I learned about him and about myself along the way.

Ebenezer

WHEN MY FRIEND LAURA was pregnant with baby number three, she did all the usual things to prepare: She made sure she had the appropriate newborn paraphernalia, she prepped her three-year-old and her one-year-old for the baby who would be joining their family, and she packed a hospital bag for herself and overnight bags for the two girls.

She had no way of knowing then that she'd need to pack not for a few days but for a few *weeks*.

Shortly after little Lowrie was born, he contracted RSV, a virus that produces cold-like symptoms in adults but can be fatal for infants. Laura stayed by his side round the clock, praying over him, worrying over him, asking the doctors questions, watching to make sure his little chest was rising and falling as it should.

In the months before Lowrie's arrival, Laura's husband had been teaching a class on 1 Samuel for the men's group at church. Just a few Sundays earlier, they had talked about the Ebenezer rock, which literally means "stone of help." (Evidently it had nothing to do with *A Christmas Carol*.) In 1 Samuel 7, the priest Samuel set up the stone as a memorial of sorts to commemorate how the Lord had intervened and given the Israelites victory over the Philistines.

"When we get out of this hospital," Laura's husband told her, "we're going to get the biggest rock we can find and put it in our yard." It would be their Ebenezer—a tangible symbol of God's faithfulness to Lowrie and to their family. They were clinging to that Ebenezer even as their son was hooked up to countless machines, tubes stuck in the crooks of his tiny arms.

As I read Laura's updates on Facebook, I was convicted about how small and, well, self-indulgent my problems were. Okay, so I had to check "1" on the RSVP for my friend's upcoming wedding, and maybe I was getting tired of spending my Friday evenings on the couch with only a bowl of Lucky Charms and a chick flick for company. But for a little perspective, my baby wasn't struggling for breath in the ICU.

Still, I wondered if maybe there was something for me to learn in this Ebenezer lesson. What would it look like for me to be faithful right where I was? Was it possible to raise my own Ebenezer as I navigated this confusing and pothole-filled world of singleness and dating? Maybe it was a meager beginning from a girl who was still wallowing in first-world dating dilemmas, but it was a start.

That evening I ventured on a walk with a singular goal: to find a handful of rocks. I couldn't set up a memorial rock in my backyard (I didn't even have a backyard, for one thing, and for another, I had no idea how my story would end yet). But maybe I could do my own version of miniature Ebenezers. Laura and her family set up a stone to mark God's faithfulness in the past; I would collect stones to mark God's faithfulness in the future.

When I got home, I found a Sharpie marker, and on the first rock I wrote "Blond Date." On the second I scrawled "The Professor," along with the dates we'd gone out. Then I put the rocks inside a little cloth pouch.

These rocks would be tangible reminders that no matter what happened, God would be faithful.

I saved the rest of the rocks for later. Heaven knew I'd need them.

My Own "Dear Abby"

IF I'D KNOWN what was in store for me when I answered my phone that Thursday afternoon, I might have done things a little differently. Like maybe not have answered at all.

The voice on the other end belonged to Dorothy. Her words whooshed out in what I've come to recognize as her no-time-to-spare-but-must-tell-you-something-important mode. And without so much as a "How are you?" she launched into a round of dreaded Find Yourself a Mate advice.

Apparently Dorothy had been listening to a TV program that afternoon, and a woman in her thirties had called in about the difficult time she and her friends were having meeting quality Christian men. The hosts offered this woman several pieces of advice, which Dorothy eagerly parroted to me:

1. Get a haircut.
2. Get a makeover.
3. Date men twenty years your senior because (and I quote), "Men your age are looking for twenty-two-year-olds."
4. Ask your friends if you have any annoying habits that make you "undateable."

A few minutes later as I hung up the phone, I could only shake my head. I knew Dorothy was sharing these gems because she cared about me and wanted only good for me, but there was still a nagging rub . . . that this poor listener had received such advice (and on the air, to boot), that it had gotten passed on to me, and ultimately that this kind of hogwash gets propagated in the first place.

Granted, there were bits of validity in the tips. Of course I should take care of myself, be open to a wide range of men, and be willing to receive constructive criticism. But I found the underlying presumption nettling: that if I hadn't found a mate yet, *it was my fault*. And for crying out loud, I was a consistent bather who made regular trips to the salon.

As if it wasn't enough to hear the pesky little voice in my head telling me I was somehow faulty goods, now this message was being broadcast over national airwaves too.

I didn't say any of this to Dorothy. But as I sat at my desk mulling over her tips, a realization barreled toward me through the side door. Maybe my problem wasn't hairstyle related, but I had to admit she was right about one thing: I could use a little more accountability in my life. If I didn't invite some people I trusted to speak truth to me, I was on the verge of reeking like week-old socks. Nobody likes to be around that kind of stink, least of all me. I figured it would be good to try to get a head start on the stench.

Preferably before The Summer of Weddings was upon me.

The Summer of Weddings

IN THE MONTHS leading up to my twenty-fifth summer, I felt as if I were living on the set of one romantic comedy after another. The only thing was, I was never in the starring role; I was always the sidekick.

The script was roughly the same each time. Boy meets girl. Boy woos girl with flowers and sweet words and romantic gestures. Boy proposes to girl. Girl invites friend to wear a color-coordinated dress at fancy ceremony. Boy and girl live happily ever after.

Then there's the part that doesn't make most of the Hollywood versions: Friend gets left behind in the marital dust.

Within the span of a few months, three of my closest people were getting married. First up was my little brother. (Red dress, strapless.) Next up was my best friend, Sarah. (Navy blue dress, empire waist.) And finally my roommate, Linnea. (Cerulean, *not* periwinkle, dress, boatneck.)

It was an honor to be asked to stand up in each of these weddings. I loved these people with every fiber of my being, and I felt confident supporting each match. And I was truly happy for all of the couples. But I was still planning to be in the restroom during the dreaded bouquet toss, if it was all the same to everyone else. And if it wasn't too much to ask, I was still holding out hope that I'd be able to find a date for the weddings and the related shenanigans. I promised God I wouldn't even care if the guy and I broke up on Labor Day, just as long as we could make it through the end of August.

My friend Mary from a book club I was part of told me she'd been in the exact same pickle when she was my age. Mary is one of the most real, most adventurous people I know (and yes, she really uses phrases like *in a pickle*). Mary probably has forty years on me, but I always feel rather boring and geriatric in her presence. She is the kind of person who, if she has trouble sleeping, will decide to drive an hour into the city at 2 a.m., just to wander around and see if anything interesting is happening. If she doesn't have plans for the upcoming week, she just might throw some things into a duffel bag and set out on an impulsive road trip from Chicago to Florida.

When I mentioned to Mary at the end of book club one evening that I was dreading showing up to all the weddings dateless, she clapped her hands together like she'd just discovered penicillin. "Doll, that one's easy!"

Apparently she'd felt the same way when her best friend got married decades ago. The only difference between the two of us was that while I thought maybe I should look into taking a Xanax, she thought I should take *action*.

"You know what I did?" Mary's grin had that trademark impish quality about it—the one I knew meant a good story was cooking. "I called an escort service."

I'm pretty sure I choked on my spiced cider. "An escort service?"

"Yeah, you know, where you hire a date for the evening."

"You hired a date for the evening?" I was aware that I was parroting back the last line of everything Mary said, but as I looked at my sixty-something friend who had bonded with me over *The Kite Runner* and *The Secret Life of Bees*, I just couldn't make my brain catch up with what I was hearing.

She let me squirm for a few more minutes before reluctantly admitting that she'd sent the guy home directly after the wedding. "But he was in the pictures, all right."

She shot me a meaningful look that I might have taken for maternal if not for the subject matter. "You should give it a shot."

Somehow I couldn't quite picture myself introducing my rent-a-boyfriend to Grandma and expecting her to believe we'd met through a friend at book club. Although I suppose in a sense that would have been true.

I decided I needed another plan for dealing with The Summer of Weddings. You know, just in case my plan A (finding a legitimate date) didn't work out and the rented eye candy was out of my price range.

I figured I needed a mentor—someone I could talk to who would help me sort things out a bit. As I considered my options, I nailed down a few key prerequisites:

1. *Must be smarter than me.* Good start, but that didn't narrow the field down much.
2. *Must be cheap—make that free—due to aforementioned bridesmaid-related expenses.* Which pretty much ruled out a real professional.
3. *Must tell me the truth.* As much I liked my friends, I was afraid they were a little too nice for the job. I was ready for some hard-core accountability.

I felt pretty good about my list, although I wasn't coming up with any possibilities yet. Then I had one of those full-body shudders as

I recalled my recent phone conversation with Dorothy. Maybe it wasn't enough for the person to be smart, cheap, and honest. I scribbled down a fourth requirement:

4. *Must be gentle.*

And suddenly the perfect person popped into my mind: Ruth, the wife of my childhood pastor. I couldn't think of anyone more gracious than Ruth. Couple that with her wisdom—not only from her knowledge of Scripture but also from raising four children in the jungles of Brazil and later living in inner-city Chicago—and I figured I had the perfect candidate.

There was just one problem: I hadn't talked to her in years. Would she remember me? Would she want to get together? And more to the point, exactly how awkward was this going to be?

So I did what I'm wont to do whenever I have a tricky call to make: I wrote myself a phone script.

I grew up with a mild case of a telephone phobia (telephobia?) that dated back to my rotary phone days, and my script-writing strategy had served me well over the years. When I was a kid, Mom used to make me call in our pizza delivery order, just for practice in phone etiquette. I hated it, but the threat of no pepperoni pizza (and the consequent wrath of my siblings) served as ample motivation.

My coping strategy was to write out every part of my side of the conversation, including potential alternate responses (noted on my script as a, b, and c), depending on what the person on the other line said. (In a cruel twist of irony, I spent an entire summer of my life doing nothing but answering phones for an orthodontist's office. I had to do away with the whole script thing the day a woman called and told me her dog had eaten her daughter's retainer and could she please get a refund. There are just some things you can't plan out, no matter how many multiple-choice options you leave yourself.)

Anyway, as gentle and as wise as Ruth was, I was also a little bit intimidated by how put together she seemed. She's the kind of person who has the china set out on her dining room table at all times—just in case someone stops by unexpectedly for supper. I was pretty sure I'd never seen her without heels, and her auburn hair was always perfectly coiffed. But then I remembered an interaction with Ruth from when I was in second grade.

It was a snowy February day, and school was canceled on account of the weather. But Mom's ladies' Bible study at Ruth's house was still on, and since Mom wasn't able to find child care in a pinch, my brother and I went along. On the slow, slushy drive there, we were coached about appropriate manners and how we needed to play quietly in another room. We were not, under any circumstances except imminent paralysis or death, to interrupt the ladies.

When we arrived at Ruth's house, the first thing I noticed was the fanciest table I'd ever seen: a burgundy tablecloth with a strip of gold running down the middle, delicate white china, and most amazing of all, *gold* flatware. I gave the room a final longing glance before Mom ushered us into the other room.

But before I could start unpacking my backpack filled with games, Ruth came over and took my brother and me by the hand. "Come here," she said. "I have special places set just for you." We followed her into the dining room, and sure enough, right in the center of the table were two places that looked just like everyone else's—with the china and gold forks and everything. But these spots also had something extra. Next to my brother's and my places were real crystal goblets filled with tiny candy hearts. My mouth gaped, and all those manners I'd been reminded about in the car evaporated before my awestruck eyes.

Thanks to Ruth, my brother and I got to eat with the ladies that morning. *And* we got candy hearts for breakfast.

Candy hearts, I told myself by way of a pep talk. *This is the lady who gave me candy hearts. It can't be so bad.* Gripping my script in one hand and the phone in the other, I took a breath and dialed, praying silently for the answering machine.

As it turned out, she answered on the first ring, and she remembered me right away. After a few pleasantries to catch up on the past decade or so, I knew I had to get to the point, but I wasn't sure how. It felt a little pretentious to ask, "Will you be my mentor?" It probably would have been more authentic to blurt out something like, "I am downright stuck in my life right now, and I want to turn out like you someday, and I was wondering if there's something you can do about it for an hour on a Saturday morning." I had a hunch that might come across as a tad desperate.

So I blathered on about how maybe we could do a Bible study together or something and how I didn't want her to feel like this was a big commitment and if at any point she didn't want to get together anymore I would totally understand.

She took all my dithering in stride. "Come over on Saturday at ten," she said.

The Manna Principle

I ARRIVED AT Ruth's house on a Saturday morning, and as I sat in my car prepping myself to go inside, it felt for all the world like a blind date. *On the bright side*, I thought, *at least we won't have that awkward dance at the end about who will pay.*

Ruth and Pastor Bob had moved out of the parsonage after he retired, but their new home was just as classy as the one I remembered visiting in second grade. When I saw the spread of "light snacks," as Ruth dismissively called them, I regretted that I'd wasted space in my stomach with that bowl of Cheerios before I came.

The coffee table between the gold-and-purple-striped overstuffed chairs was laden with a delectable spread: enormous red grapes in a crystal bowl, croissants, and assorted European dark chocolates. And of course, the famous gold flatware. The aroma of hazelnut coffee wafted into the room from the kitchen nearby.

But with the nervous pit in my stomach, I wasn't sure I'd be able to eat a bite. How would we even begin?

When I brought up the idea of doing a study together, Ruth just smiled her gracious smile and said, "After all these years, I really like to do things serendipity style."

"Serendipity style?" Was this some kind of new trend for Bible studies I hadn't heard about? I racked my brain, trying to figure out what she was talking about.

"Yes, serendipity—just going along and making delightful, unexpected discoveries on the way." Then with a wink she said, "I'm getting too old for lots of structure and studies and fill in the blanks."

And so we didn't have a program or a book or a road map. We just sat down and drank our coffee and talked. Or rather, *I* talked. It wasn't long before I forgot about Ruth's perfect china and flawless hair and poised composure, and I spilled all my fears about The Summer of Weddings. How I was afraid that my friends would find couple friends and move on without me. How I was afraid my best friend would now have someone else to share her hopes and dreams with and I'd just be an afterthought. How I was worried about being the third wheel after my roommate got married. How I never imagined my little brother would beat me to the altar and how I dreaded the family questions about when it would be my turn. How I was afraid to live by myself after my roommate moved out—or maybe not so much afraid to live alone as afraid of being lonely. How I wondered if God had overlooked me when he was doling out the spousal blessings.

I took a breath, and suddenly I was ravenous. I heaped a pile of grapes and chocolates on my plate. I snuck a glance at Ruth, wondering why I'd been so nervous. Her face was the picture of grace, and she didn't seem the least bit put off by my blathering. It felt like I'd just invited a houseguest to peek into the closet where I'd crammed everything in a tornadic heap before her arrival. It's not so much that I was afraid she'd think less of me, but that I wasn't sure I was ready to open myself up to this level of exposure.

When Ruth spoke, her response wasn't at all what I'd expected. I guess I figured she'd give me some tips from the World of the Married—how I should empathize with my friends, or take on some pointers about being a good bridesmaid. But Ruth got right to the core of things.

"Do you remember the story about manna, when Moses was leading the Israelites through the desert?" she asked.

I looked at the croissant in my hand. *Where is she going with this?* I was pretty sure I'd just finished a discourse about twenty-first-century weddings, not ancient Middle Eastern history.

"Um, yeah," I said. "I'm pretty sure Pastor Bob did some flannelgraph stories about that."

"Something that I've always found fascinating about that account is the one-day rule." She started flipping through the pages of her worn Bible. "God gave the Israelites exactly the provision they needed for that day. But the moment they tried to hoard it and store some up for the future, it became moldy."

She turned to Exodus, to chapter 16. "Here it is. 'When they measured it out, everyone had just enough. . . . Then Moses told them, "Do not keep any of it until morning." But some of them didn't listen and kept some of it until morning. But by then it was full of maggots and had a terrible smell'" (verses 18-19).

Ruth looked at me. "It seems to me that God doesn't usually give us enough grace for a whole summer all at once. Otherwise, knowing us, we'd start thinking we could handle things on our own. If we didn't have to come to him daily for our provision, we'd forget how desperately we need him."

∽

When I got home after picking up a few things at the store, my stomach still felt stuffed after all those "light snacks." Come to think of it, my soul felt fuller than it had in a while too.

I opened the pantry door, still thinking about Ruth's words about manna, and it hit me that I had a pantry problem. And a freezer problem too, for that matter.

I guess you could blame it on the fact that I come from an ancestral line of farming women who knew how to can and pickle and pantrify and store up for winter with the best of them. Even today, if you went to my grandma's house, you'd find a stuffed freezer upstairs, plus another full freezer and a huge Deepfreeze in the basement—all of them stocked with homemade goodies.

I missed the farming and canning gene, but I sure got the freezer gene.

If I don't have a backup of everything in the pantry, and if my freezer door can close without heroic efforts, I start getting vaguely antsy. I realize I live in the era of Costco, not *Little House on the Prairie*, but I can't seem to stop myself.

Maybe, I pondered, *my pantry is just the visible proof of a deeper spiritual neurosis.* The stocked pantry was evidence of my desire to control my own life, to seek a sense of security. I wanted to hoard grace—stockpile it, stash a backup supply just behind the canned green beans. Maybe the things I wanted and thought I needed weren't bad in themselves. My problem, in the words of Gregory the Great, was that I was grabbing after them "too soon, too delicately, too expensively, too greedily, too much."

The story goes that Abba Poemen, who predated Gregory by a couple of centuries and was considered by scholars to be the quintessential desert father, was asked who Jesus was speaking to when he gave the command about not being anxious about tomorrow (Matthew 6:34). The old man replied, "It is said for the person who is tempted and has little strength, so that such a person may not worry, saying within: 'How long must I suffer this temptation?' That person should rather say each day: 'Just today.'"[1]

The days of manna in the desert may have been over, but maybe the principle still applied. "I know you," God seemed to be saying, "and I know that if you stored away my provision, you would forget the one who gave it to you in the first place. I will give you the grace you need. Just enough for today."

Out of nowhere, the Lord's Prayer started bubbling out of me, right there in the pantry. I hadn't thought much about the "Our Father" in a while, since the church I attended was more into extemporaneous types of prayer. But I used to say it every Sunday at church as a kid, led by Pastor Bob's sonorous voice. It was all still there.

> Our Father, who art in heaven
> Hallowed be thy name . . .

When I got to this line, my oxygen supply ceased midsentence:

> Give us today our daily bread.

It was as if I were hearing these words for the first time.

Apparently Jesus was onto the Manna Principle too. When he taught his followers how to pray, he didn't tell them to ask for food for the years to come or even to cover this week's groceries. He instructed them to ask for today. Just today.

Maybe it's the same with grace. He gives us just what we need for today. And that's enough. Even for days with other people's weddings in them.

Thrice a Bridesmaid

To my amazement, The Summer of Weddings went off without a hitch. So to speak.

Admittedly, however, there were a few minor meltdowns. Like the day before my brother's wedding, when Grandma and I were running some last-minute errands for ice and yet another strand of tiny white lights. While we were en route, she mentioned casually that my little cousin Jenny had harbored secret dreams of being a flower girl, but now that she was ten, she was afraid she was too old for the job. Apparently Grandma had explained to her in no uncertain terms that if I'd gotten married when I should have, Jen could have been my flower girl.

Grandma had a twinkle in her eye when she said it, but the comment still stung. She had done a lot of wonderful grandmothering over the years, from making me a homemade Care Bear (with a tiny heart stitched on the backside) to sewing me my favorite velour shirt to treating me to her mouthwatering desserts, which were famous across the county. So with those memories at the forefront of my mind, and with the knowledge that it's largely considered bad form to hurt old ladies, especially your grandmother, I let the comment slide.

And there were lighter moments too, like watching my dad in a tux for the first time in his life, squirming like a kid who has been sitting still in church too long. Through my laughter, I made a solemn promise that should the day ever come for me, I'd let him wear whatever he wanted to wear to my wedding. Even his beloved grungy basketball T-shirt.

On the way to the church, I gave a ride to my cousin Jenny (she of the thwarted flower girl aspirations) and her six-year-old brother, Lucas, the ring bearer, who had done some serious soul-searching before committing to the job. Ultimately he'd agreed, telling my brother, "I promised my dad I'd be a pilot when I grow up, but I've thought about it, and I'll be your ring bearer instead."

As it turned out, there's nothing like having the company of two spunky kids to provide the grace of distraction. Somewhere during a break in our lively conversations about semitrucks and the Jonas Brothers, I heard some lines to the song "Faithful," and it felt like God was tossing me a buoy in these unpredictable wedding waters. I might be going to the wedding dateless, but I wasn't alone.

> *I have found nothing but good in your heart . . .*
> *I know you'll never leave, leave me alone.*[1]

I clung to those words about God's faithfulness throughout the ceremony and the picture taking and the reception, and as the evening came to a close, I looked back and realized in amazement that there had been manna enough. Yes, Kyle was married now, but he was still my brother, and he always would be. And to sweeten the deal, I had a new sister.

And on that day, there wasn't just manna. There was also cake.

The night of the wedding, our extended family stayed in town, and the cousins had a slumber party at my place. The grown-ups were all coming over for coffee in the morning to see my condo.

Jenny and I couldn't sleep that night. She was still wired with sugar and on West Coast time, and I was kept up by a mind still awhirl, trying to wrap my head around the fact that my little brother was officially, irrevocably, 100 percent married.

"Hey, Jen. Are you still awake?"

"Yeah," she whispered back.

"I have an idea. You've been wanting to be a flower girl, right? How about we make that happen tomorrow?"

A beat of silence from the direction of the sleeping bag. "Um . . . okay!"

And so the next morning I pulled out my big box of dress-up clothes, complete with my mom's outfits from the seventies, a few outrageous eighties numbers of my own, and the bridesmaid dresses from all the weddings I'd been in, including the red strapless one from the day before.

When Grandma and Grandpa and the aunts and uncles came over, Jenny and I hosted our very own fashion show. I played the part of the emcee, and Jen was the runway model, donning each dress and alternately posing and cracking up into fits of giggles. The adults snapped picture after picture—possibly enough to qualify her for true flower girl status.

I'd venture to say even Grandma was smiling.

~∞~

A couple of months later I flew to Seattle for my friend Sarah's wedding. I'd recently started a new job at a book-publishing company, but one of the conditions when I accepted was that I'd be able to take off the week before Sarah's wedding. It was hard to be a good maid of honor from three thousand miles away.

When I arrived, there was still plenty to do: put the programs together, make last-minute phone calls, book final travel arrangements, and run interference when people were getting a little too demanding of the bride's time. By the end of the week, Sarah and her fiancé, Seth, had dubbed me Stephretary, and that made me happy. My friend might be moving into a different life-stage bracket, but she still needed me.

Best of all, though, Sarah and I were able to talk and pray together at night after a day of Wedding Central, just like we'd done back when we were college roommates. Each night back in the dorm, we'd lie in our bunk beds, whispering long past bedtime about our dreams for the future—falling in love, getting dream jobs, traveling the world, going to Italy. We'd talk about the things that worried us, the things that haunted us. Most of all, we prayed for the husbands God might have in mind for us, that he would protect them and make them into the men he wanted them to be.

Now, as Sarah's wedding approached, we talked about what our friendship would look like with a guy in the mix. I told her that I was scared I'd become superfluous once she had a confidant who also happened to live at her house. She countered that it wouldn't be fair to expect one man to fill the role of husband and best girlfriend.

And we prayed, like old times, but now in Sarah's case, we had a name for her husband-to-be.

The day of the wedding dawned bright and sunny, and my eyes leaked all the way through the ceremony. But it was okay because, to my surprise, they weren't just tears of loss. There were also tears of joy mixed in. Seth was indeed the answer to our prayers.

And besides, I'd had the foresight to wear waterproof mascara.

After the wedding I took a red-eye flight home, and I was exhausted but content as I made my way through the security line.

For no logical reason, I always feel vaguely guilty whenever I walk through the scanning machine, certain the screeners will find something about me that hints at terrorist tendencies and I'll be pulled aside for a thorough grilling. As a result, I'm fairly obsessed with emptying my person of all metal long before I get to the airport.

But the careful de-metaling was to no avail—the beeping started the moment my foot crossed the threshold of the full-body scanner. The security guard pulled me aside and started firing questions at me, ordering me to empty my pockets (already empty) and remove my jewelry (already removed).

By the time the guard pulled out the handheld scanner, her suspicion was clearly growing. She waved the little machine all over my body in the usual places. Nothing. Then she raised the scanner to my head, and all at once the room was filled with incessant beeping. You'd have thought a whole fleet of trucks were simultaneously backing up.

As every eye in the security line turned in my direction, it suddenly hit me. The bobby pins—approximately 350 of them—all on top of my head. With all that had happened that day, I'd forgotten about the professional updo I'd been sporting since that morning.

The security woman called over her supervisor. Meanwhile, I had visions of having to remove all 350 of the bobby pins right there in the security line, after which I'd be guaranteed to miss my plane and have a terminal full of travelers staring at the girl with the rat's nest atop her head.

Fortunately the supervisor had mercy on a poor bridesmaid, and I was allowed to board the plane with my updo intact. As I settled into my seat, it occurred to me that maybe God allots grace in daily serving sizes precisely because of situations like this one. If I were to budget out how much grace I'd need in advance, I'd always end up way off, never remembering to ration out enough for those pesky bobby pins. The things I obsess over and worry about most often don't happen at all, and the things I need grace for I never even see coming.

That was about the extent of my deep thoughts before I was fast asleep. Not even 350 metal clips could keep my eyes open after a day as full as that.

∾

Next up was my roommate Linnea's wedding. She'd be moving out of my condo once she got married, which meant I'd be losing her company *and* her rent. We'd lived on the same wing in college, but we really became friends during our years of living in the COTTAGE, as we dubbed our place, when we were both teachers in the same school district. I'm pretty sure we intended the name to be an acronym for something, but we never quite nailed down what all the letters stood for.

Linnea's fiancé, John, had become a fairly regular fixture at our place, and from the moment he came up with the idea for the two of them to show up at a costume party as a math test and an answer key, I knew he was perfect for my math-teacher friend. (Granted, he had some other more substantial qualities, but the matching sweatshirts kind of sealed it.)

I was going to miss Linnea and our daily Fifteen Minutes of Fun—the system we'd worked out for two responsible types who without intervention would end up spending all evening grading papers or being otherwise productive. Sometimes our Fifteen Minutes of Fun involved making a quick trip to the grocery store to purchase the most exotic fruit we could find or fixing microwave s'mores or planning an invented holiday as an excuse to invite people over the next weekend. That fifteen-minute window of fun was small, but it meant something big.

On a Saturday after one of Linnea's wedding showers, we were sitting on the kitchen floor, sorting pots and pans and dishes. After living in the same place for several years, we couldn't quite remember what belonged to whom. And now there was Linnea's registry to consider. I think we were addressing the Tupperware shelf when I started blubbering. My words came out in what must have sounded like an emotional tumble to my logical, left-brained friend—something to the effect of "I'm going to miss hanging out with you, and I don't know if I can live by myself, and to top it all off you get the husband *and* the brand-new dishes."

I was horrified when I heard myself say the words out loud. But Linnea's response surprised me even more. As eager as she was to marry John, there were some parts of this new life stage that would feel like a loss for her too. *Really? She would miss me? Even with all those fancy new dishes?*

Well, knock me over with a strand of tulle.

In my personal pity shower, it had never crossed my mind that I wasn't the only one who had a right to grieve certain endings, even ones that were good and right and holy.

When I stood up at Linnea and John's wedding, I was struck by the lyrics to the song John's friends sang just before the couple said their vows:

> *We stand as witness to a miracle*
> *Of the two becoming one*[2]

And I realized that I wasn't just the leftovers here; I had an important role to play. I wasn't there just to wear a cerulean dress and smile for a marathon photo session and be on the receiving end of secondhand Tupperware containers. I was there as a witness. I was there to share in and tell about the gracious work God was doing in and through this couple. And that job wasn't ending today; it was just beginning.

The evening came to a close, and I joined the other guests to send Linnea and John off. While they drove away, I offered some final words to John: "She'll make a good roommate!"

I had made it through The Summer of Weddings. And I hadn't even needed to resort to the escort service.

For Sale by Owner

After Linnea moved out, I decided to put my house on the market and move closer to my new job. I'd never had aspirations to climb the corporate ladder. I was much more focused on having a family, and acquiring pantsuits in various shades had never been on my radar. But this job was special—it was something I believed in, something I was passionate about, something that aligned with my gifts and vision. I loved working on manuscripts, first as a copyeditor, wrangling commas and checking facts and polishing sentences until they gleamed, and gradually dabbling in the bigger-picture, content-level world of editing. I was ready to go all in. It was time to move.

I made it through the whole real estate ordeal with only two meltdowns, which under the circumstances struck me as downright heroic.

The first breakdown occurred right in the middle of the Home Depot aisle, where I was purchasing a "For Sale by Owner" sign and an accompanying wooden stake to secure it in the ground.

Dad had convinced me that it would be no problem to do this myself, and I believed him, with the proviso that he'd come over at a moment's notice if a scary-sounding guy knocked on the door and wanted to look at the place.

I'm not quite sure what it was about the sign aisle that set me off, but most likely it was merely the final nudge in one of those cumulative cries—the avalanche that's triggered by one fateful snowflake. If you'd come across me in the Home Depot aisle that day (mercifully, no one did), I wouldn't have been able to articulate anything coherent about why I was riffling through my purse for a ratty tissue, but it likely would have been something like this: "My roommate got married and moved out and I'm going to miss this place and I wish I had a guy to pound this sign into the ground for me, not to mention stand in as my personal bouncer when random strangers come into my place." Or if you were looking for the shorter version, it would have sounded more like: "If I had a man, I wouldn't be stuck in this situation right now."

The good news was that the first person to look at my place bought it. And he was neither a stalker nor a serial killer, which seemed auspicious. Even so, I almost refused to sell the condo to him. Here's why: I wasn't sure he could be deemed worthy of the fond memories that echoed in those walls from the years Linnea and I had lived there. After touring the first floor, he asked the price and said, "It's cheaper than the other place I was looking at. I'll take it."

I stared at him, mouth agape. "Don't you want to at least go upstairs?" I gripped my keys until they left a jagged mark on my hand.

"Nah, that's all right. These places all look pretty much the same."

No way. I would not sell this place—this home—to some ungrateful oaf who didn't even want to look at the bedrooms.

Eventually, though, practicality won out, and I inked the deal.

Against my better judgment, I even scrubbed the place clean before I moved, all the while muttering invectives against this guy who would never love this place as much as I had.

⟡

The town house I moved in to . . . well, let's just say it fell into the "has potential" category. I'd never imagined buying a place to live in on my own. Could I really do this solo? That question was put to the test from the day I moved in.

When I arrived on the day of the closing, I was shocked to discover that the family who lived there hadn't packed the majority of their belongings yet. I wasn't even able to get into the house until five hours after the agreed-upon time. Complicating matters, I'd closed on my old place the same day and had the U-Haul for twenty-four hours, so everything needed to be unloaded that evening.

When the old owners finally left and I was able to go inside, I felt like I was entering a crime scene. Piles of junk were littered throughout the place—assorted dishes, unwanted knickknacks and decorations, piles of unvacuumed dog hair, and what ultimately totaled up to fourteen bags full of trash.

I sat on the stairs, the only place uncluttered with boxes and junk, and despaired that this place would never feel like home.

Fortunately, that's about when my mom showed up. She just happens to be the best possible person to have on your side for any stateside emergency, and you can count on her to have a plan of attack within moments. But first there was an even more important order of business: We went into each room and said a prayer of blessing over each one.

Our prayers cast a vision for what we couldn't yet see with our eyes. We asked God to make the living room a place of warmth and laughter, to make the kitchen a place where people were fed and where memorable conversations happened. In the guest room, we asked God to make it a place of hospitality for friends and visitors. In my bedroom we asked that it be a place of rest and peace and refreshment. (I added a silent prayer for passionate marital sex to happen there someday too, but didn't voice that in front of my mom. That just would have been weird.)

And soon enough, one by one, my people started coming. I'd asked them to help me unload the truck; I'd had no idea that this was what I'd find when I arrived. I was so involved with directing traffic and funneling boxes and showing people where things went that I didn't really know what everyone was up to. So when I finally took a break to size up the damage, I was shocked by what I saw. It felt like one of those George Bailey moments—one minute you're contemplating jumping off a snowy bridge, and the next you've discovered that your friends have rallied together with enough heroic efforts to make you want to live again.

I peeked into the upstairs bathroom and saw my aunt, her sleeves rolled up, scrubbing the toilet. Two of my friends were in the guest room, unloading box after box of books (and never once complaining about the ridiculous book-to-person ratio in the place). My mom's head was deep in the oven, muscling off a decade of grime and grease. My dad was on one end of the sofa bed that was being carried upstairs—the one that was so heavy he'd previously sworn he'd never move it again. My uncle was removing garbage bags full of trash left by the previous owners. Another friend was on her way to get dinner for the whole crew.

In that moment, I had a revelation. Home is not a place. It's not something you can sell to an apathetic guy via a wobbly-staked Home Depot sign. Home is relationship. Even if I had nowhere to lay my head that night, I had *home*—not only from these people who showed up with tangible love, but even more so from the God who invites us to dwell in him. The early church father Origen put it best: "May he be my ground, he my house, he my mansion, he my repose, and may he be the place where I dwell."[1]

Home was here, written all over the faces of these people who loved me and even more, on the heart of the God who promises to be our shelter and place of safety. Before I collapsed into my bed that night, the words from this psalm rang in my ears:

> Lord, through all the generations
>   you have been our home!
> Before the mountains were born,
>   before you gave birth to the earth and the world,
>   from beginning to end, you are God.
>
> PSALM 90:1-2

No matter how adrift I felt, I would always have a place to put down roots, a place to lay my head. I would always have home.

The Anti-Loneliness Campaign

A FRIEND OF MINE once told me there are three types of friends. First there are Christmas Card Friends—the ones you'd like to see a photo of each year to find out how many kids they have and if they got a dog or a new haircut, but that's sufficient. Then there are 7-Eleven Friends—the ones who are convenient and available to hang out with, but you probably wouldn't call them at 2 a.m. And finally there are Kidney Donor Friends—the ones you'd give one of your kidneys to, should the need arise.

Those distinctions took on new meaning once I'd been living on my own at my new place for a few weeks. After more than my share of general moping and ringing up astronomical electric bills (I'd made a habit of leaving on all the lights in the house in an attempt to scare away would-be bogeymen), I decided something needed to change. But change, even good change, is a scary proposition. So I made a tactical maneuver: I launched a campaign instead. I dubbed my little program the ALC: the Anti-Loneliness Campaign.

The premise was simple. I knew that anytime I was feeling low, I tended to get a case of emotional amnesia and forget all the people who loved me. So I put a list on my refrigerator with names on it—people who agreed to let me call them anytime, night or day, in a real crisis or in an imagined crisis or for no reason at all. I went so far as to make these long-suffering individuals sign my refrigerator covenant. Then whenever I heard the whispers that I was utterly alone, that no one loved me, those signatures would tell another story.

One night in college, Sarah and I were up late talking as usual when the conversation meandered to our favorite people in the Bible. Sarah, with her creative, musical bent and her ability to feel things deeply, resonated with David. The psalmist. The man after God's own heart (see Acts 13:22). My favorite had always been the unsung Jonathan, who played a smaller part in the Old Testament but was made of the true-blue loyalty I aspired to. It smacked of destiny that these two guys who were our favorites also happened to be best friends on the pages of Scripture.

The ALC seemed like an auspicious time to take another look at the story of David and Jonathan. If anyone was in need of a faithful, kidney-level friend, it was David. He'd had his share of successes—killing a giant, notching up some significant battle victories, and being anointed the future king of Israel. But now the current king, Saul, was trying to kill him, and David was forced to flee the very country he was supposed to rule someday.

In something of an ironic twist, it was Saul's son—the heir apparent—who showed David true friendship. More than once Jonathan saved his friend's life—risking his own royal neck and effectively handing over the crown that should have been his. In his reckoning, friendship trumped safety, personal advancement, even the keys to his dad's kingdom. "Jonathan made David reaffirm his vow of friendship again, for Jonathan loved David as he loved himself" (1 Samuel 20:17).

If David had had a refrigerator, I had no doubt Jonathan would have posted his vow of friendship there.

One of the unexpected perks of the ALC, aside from discovering that I really did have Kidney Donor Friends, was the way their faithfulness reminded me of God's faithfulness. In the moments I couldn't see God's steadfastness or feel his love, these people were tangible proof that God had my back.

The same seemed to be true for David. After he and Jonathan said their good-byes, David fled from Saul and hid in a cave. From there he wrote a heart-wrenching psalm about the enemies who had set a trap for him and how weary he was. But shortly thereafter his psalm turns a corner:

> My heart is confident in you, O God;
>   my heart is confident.
>   No wonder I can sing your praises!
>
> PSALM 57:7

I have to wonder if it was Jonathan's friendship, at least in part, that helped David believe God hadn't left him after all.

I hoped I would never need to call in a kidney favor from one of my friends. But I wasn't alone. And I had the piece of paper on my refrigerator to prove it.

PART 3

Community

When the love of God is completely overwhelming,
it binds the lover not just to God
but to everyone else too.

THALASSIOS THE LIBYAN

Uber-Fundamentalist Boy

BEFORE I MET blind date number three, I had to go through what amounted to a theological interrogation.

This blind date had been arranged by another friend from work. It took some prodding for me to say yes—I was a little gun-shy after the last work-related matchmaking didn't pan out. That was one piece I hadn't thought through completely: When a third party is involved, there's potential for yet another person to get hurt or feel bad.

The coworker who had set me up with The Professor had been utterly gracious and understanding, but it was sobering to realize that the stakes were higher than just the blind date and me. A flop (from either perspective) could mean a breakup of another sort for the matchmaker. I was wary of intentionally putting myself—and another coworker—in this situation again.

"So tell me what you know about this guy," I said. I hoped we had more in common than just *Hey, here are two single people I know!*

"Well, he's serious about his faith," he said. "I think you'd have a lot to talk about."

That was a start. Besides, my friend's wife had also met this guy and agreed this was a good idea. I didn't know her, but it helped to have her objective vote of confidence. Besides, my coworker said, "Don't worry—you never have to follow up with me either way." So, sucking in a gulp of oxygen, I passed along my contact information.

At first I naively assumed that the phone number exchange through our mutual friend was for the purpose of engaging in introductory chitchat and making logistical arrangements, but I soon realized it was so my date could conduct something of an ecclesiastical screening.

We'd barely gotten past our hellos and introductions when Uber-Fundamentalist Boy waded into some deep doctrinal waters. Did I think Catholics, Lutherans, and Presbyterians could make it to heaven, despite their shaky belief systems? What was my stance on infant baptism? And what was the Holy Spirit's role in Communion— was I in the transubstantiation camp or the ordinance camp?

Uber-Fundamentalist Boy did little to mask his horror at my dubious theological leanings (in particular, my conviction that Mother Teresa and my faithful Catholic grandparents loved the same Jesus I love).

I'm still not sure why he agreed to meet me after uncovering my heresies. Who knows—perhaps he thought he'd be able to convert me to his leanings in person. Whatever his motivation, I was a bit surprised at the end of the conversation when he asked if I'd like to meet him at Panera that Friday. I was perhaps even more surprised to hear myself say yes.

I got out my Sharpie and etched "Uber-Fundamentalist Boy" on another Ebenezer rock. As I dropped it in the bag, I whispered a prayer that God would show himself faithful—whatever that would look like.

I had done my homework in the conversation department this time. Not wanting to get stuck without any conversational tennis balls, I got a yellow Post-it, wrote down a few topics we could talk about, and stuck it in my purse. I figured I could surreptitiously sneak peeks at it if we found ourselves in a conversation lull. Here were some of my aces in the hole: "summer plans," "how you ended up in Illinois," "what your hometown is like."

But from the moment we sat down in our booth, it was clear he had some other topics in mind:

"Do you think you should you listen to your boss if he's not a Christian?" he asked.

"Um, I feel like I need more context," I said.

"Do you think you should attend a wedding if the couple isn't spiritually mature enough?"

"Uhh . . ." How had we skipped over icebreaker questions and gone straight into deep theological thoughts? I never thought I'd find myself wishing for small talk.

I realized that the biggest hurdle we had here wasn't necessarily where we landed on these theological stumpers or whether we agreed. The question was how we communicated about them—and how safe I felt to be myself. I was confident there was a woman out there who would enjoy this kind of theological haranguing, but I was pretty sure that woman wasn't me.

As I sat there sipping my iced tea, something occurred to me that should have been obvious long ago. I'd been coasting along for years under the assumption that being with someone would ensure that I wouldn't feel alone anymore. That being with someone would mean I'd be seen and known. That I'd be loved. But after an evening of being with Uber-Fundamentalist Boy, I knew without a doubt that that was no guarantee.

About a week after the flopped blind date, I was at a going-away party at a friend's house, and my matchmaker and his wife were there. I hadn't debriefed the date with him at all—partly because our cubicle wall offered zero privacy, but more to the point, I wasn't sure what I'd say even if I got up the gumption to eke out some words. It wasn't his fault that the date had gone down the way it had, and I didn't want him to feel responsible.

But there was no way around it now: This was awkward. There was a big blind elephant in the room, and somehow it felt more obtrusive now that we were outside work. Everyone at the party went around and introduced themselves, and after I finished, my coworker promptly whispered something in his wife's ear.

I felt my neck breaking out in red splotches, and I was sure the whole room knew the secret: "That's the blind date girl!"

I was back on the hot seat, only this time Uber-Fundamentalist Boy wasn't the one grilling me; instead, I felt like a dozen pairs of eyes were sizing me up. There was only one remaining course of action: quit my job, assume a new identity, and move to New Zealand.

A Scattered Shower

A FEW MONTHS AFTER Linnea had moved out, I invited her over to celebrate her birthday with me. It was my first winter living alone, and I was glad for the company and the chance to breathe life into the walls of my quiet place. Just as Linnea was getting ready to head home, my doorbell rang. *Weird*, I thought. *Nobody ever just shows up at my door.*

I opened the door, inviting a gust of cold air to blast inside. A big guy I'd never seen before was standing on my top porch step. "Do you want to buy a vacuum cleaner?" he asked.

I declined, but he persisted.

Then Linnea came out of the living room and into Vacuum Guy's view. The moment he saw her, he jumped backward off the step and bolted into the windowless van waiting on the street.

I closed the door, trying to process all the pieces. "Linnea," I said, "he didn't have any literature with him. And he didn't even have a uniform, let alone a vacuum."

Ever a woman of action, Linnea said, "Let's see if he stopped at any of your neighbors' houses."

We threw on our jackets and hopped in the car, searching the neighborhood for the white van. It was nowhere in sight.

I was officially freaked out. After several sleepless nights of leaving all the lights on and hearing noises that were probably my dishwasher (but I was sure were the sounds of a serial killer jimmying the lock), I figured I should call the police and give them a friendly heads-up that an ax murderer posing as a vacuum cleaner salesman was roaming the neighborhood.

The woman who answered my call sounded utterly bored, despite the fact that my voice was probably registering on a Richter scale somewhere. "Well, if this had just happened, I could do something about it. But as it is, there's really nothing I can do." I could have sworn she was chomping gum as she talked to me. Maybe even filing her nails.

So much for that idea. And so much for lowering my electricity bill.

When our small group met next, I debated whether I should mention my insomnia and recurring white van–related nightmares. It seemed so silly in the light of day, especially when everyone else had real things to worry about, like dealing with the heartbreak of another potential adoption that had fallen through, a brother who was going through a serious rough patch, and a good friend who had cancer.

But finally one week I managed to squeak out my lame-sounding request—that I felt scared and vulnerable and alone, and what if Vacuum Guy had come when I was home by myself?

Thankfully my small group friends weren't nearly as condescending as the nonemergency police receptionist, and they empathized with my fears (even the irrational ones). Despite my natural tendency to request prayer for anyone but myself and my desire to look like

I could pull off my single-woman life with the best of the Carrie Bradshaws, I felt lighter having gotten it off my chest.

But there was no way I could have predicted what happened the next week.

When I arrived at small group, something in the air seemed odd, like someone had put a whoopee cushion under my chair and they were just waiting for me to sit down. Then, as if on cue, everyone started pulling out packages—some wrapped and others in plastic bags. I racked my brain—Christmas had passed, it wasn't my birthday . . . what was going on?

"Open them!" they said, ignoring my befuddlement.

It wasn't a bridal shower or a baby shower like I'd always imagined, but this was a shower all right—a Single-Girl Protection shower. I opened the bags to discover alarms to put on my windows that would go off if someone tried to break in, a metal bar that could be jammed under my bedroom door to keep out would-be intruders, and night-lights for my peace of mind. My friends had thought of everything.

When I got home and crawled into bed that night, I cried. But this time it wasn't out of fear; it was out of gratitude. And for the first time in a long time, under the glow of my little blue night-light, I slept like a baby.

Are You My Neighbor?

WHEN I BROUGHT chocolate chip cookies next door to the new neighbors, it was a far cry from altruism. Mostly it was just that I'd made a bargain with God. He'd done his part, so I figured the least I could do in return was a little baking. I knew that's not how he operates, but still.

The thing is, the guy who had lived next door made me nervous. Nothing worthy of calling the police about . . . just enough to give me a certifiable case of the heebie-jeebies.

I'd wake up in the middle of the night to Neighbor Guy's TV blaring through our shared wall. Worse than the decibel level of whatever awful rerun was on at 2 a.m., however, was the unmistakable sound of Neighbor Guy's voice throwing in his own obscenities over the racket. On afternoons when the weather was nice, he'd sit on his porch and rant into his phone. I don't have the medical background to prove this, but I'm pretty sure it's not healthy for someone's neck veins to bulge quite that much.

So I told God that if he'd get a U-Haul into Neighbor Guy's driveway and move him out, I'd be a good neighbor to whoever moved in next.

I shouldn't have been so surprised when, a few months later, I saw a moving truck in the driveway next door. I may have even danced a little jig right there in the entryway, celebrating Neighbor Guy's abrupt departure. But then it hit me: *Oh yeah. That means it's time to step up and be a good neighbor.* I hadn't really thought through what it would look like to make good on my end of the bargain, but one of my life philosophies is that cookies are a pretty safe solution for just about any iffy situation. I snatched a cookie off the plate and scarfed it down for courage before knocking on the new neighbors' door.

When it opened, I was hit by a bustling wave of humanity. Someone was unpacking dishes in the kitchen, boxes were being carried up the stairs, and in every corner of the town house, people were laughing and talking. No one was speaking in English, but I figured chocolate chip cookies wouldn't require much translation.

After meeting a string of people, I was finally introduced to Blanca and Rodrigo, my new neighbors. My no-yelling-on-the-patio neighbors, or so I hoped. It turned out Blanca spoke three languages fluently, and her handle on English often put my own vocabulary to shame. We discovered that we had some similarities—I was a former teacher and Blanca was on the road to becoming one. We both loved movies, our families, and trying new foods.

But there were some significant differences, too. I ate dinner around 6:00; Blanca didn't even start cooking until about 9:00. She grew up in a place where the temperature rarely dropped below 70; I'd spent winters praying for snow days as a kid. I was recovering from what I thought were considerable bridesmaid duties, but they paled in comparison to what Blanca was expected to do for her sister's wedding in Monterrey—a several-day affair, with new outfits required for each day.

Although our first conversation (and the cookies, apparently) had gone over well, I wasn't quite sure how to have a real neighbor . . . or to be one. When ranting Neighbor Guy had lived next door, I'd gotten into the habit of opening my garage door and slipping inside without making contact. And honestly, it was easier that way. As an introvert, I found it less taxing to skulk in through the garage than to drum up conversation with people I barely knew.

Then came the Sunday I heard a sermon about the "Who is my neighbor?" passage. As Pastor Dave read Luke 10, I'd already started to ponder my lunch options for that day. Banana pancakes or three-cheese omelet? I'd heard probably a dozen sermons on that parable, and I was confident I knew it all: Your neighbor isn't so much the person who lives in close proximity to you; it's the person in need, the guy on the side of the metaphorical road. Show love to him, and you're showing love to God. Check, check, and check.

Then Pastor Dave said something that jarred me out of my culinary musings: "What about your actual neighbors . . . the people who live on your street? Do you know them? Would you even recognize them if you passed them on the side of the road as you're riding your donkey?" Oh. I'd prefer to go back to considering the merits of cheese, please.

And then the questions grew even more squirm-inducing: "Would you be the person your neighbors would call if they'd been robbed and were lying on the side of the road?" It was much easier to accept the passage when *neighbor* meant a vague needy person I'd never met. It was a lot more convicting when I had to conjure up a mental picture to accompany the definition.

Blanca and Rodrigo certainly weren't needy, but despite all the friends who had come in from out of town to help them move in, they were far from home, far from family, far from community. And

I was their neighbor. Augustine pointed out that while the love of God is the first and greatest commandment mentioned in Matthew 22, loving our neighbor comes in as a close second. "You cannot yet see God," he said. "It is in loving your neighbor that you grow worthy to see God; only by loving your neighbor can you polish your eyes to see God."[1]

Thus began my adventure in cross-cultural friendship. Blanca and I had some humorous moments of miscommunication: my trying to explain that *sister-in-law* can mean husband's sister *or* brother's wife, her trying to come up with the English word *mayonnaise*—a process that felt like a chaotic mix of Taboo and charades. We ate dinner together on occasion and laughed at my bland chicken recipes and their affinity for putting cayenne pepper on a perfectly sweet coconut.

We watched movies together . . . some in Spanish with English subtitles, some in English with Spanish subtitles. We talked about the upsides and downsides of our respective religious upbringings. And when Blanca and Rodrigo decided to give church a try again after a seven-year hiatus, the three of us decided to go together.

We went to the rock-and-roll Spanish church, where I caught only a few words here and there. (I did perk up mid-sermon when the pastor mentioned something about burritos.) Then we went to an old-school mass in English, which felt foreign to me in its own way, with the holy water and kneeling benches and ceremonial laps with the Holy Scriptures.

And there was the time Blanca and Rodrigo celebrated their first American Thanksgiving with me and my extended family, complete with turkey, mashed potatoes, pumpkin pie, football, and my family's tradition of using fabric markers to write what we were thankful for on the special Thanksgiving tablecloth.

On the path from next-door acquaintances to real neighbors, something surprising happened: It became easier to reach out to other people on our street. With the buttressing that came with having a core, it wasn't quite as scary to have a neighborhood cookout, to bring cookies around at Christmastime, to get some of the women together once a month to try out new restaurants in our area.

When Blanca announced that she was pregnant, it seemed only appropriate to celebrate with the little group from our neighborhood. As everyone oohed over tiny pink outfits and itty-bitty ballerina shoes and exclaimed over her sonogram pictures, I gazed around the room with a surge of gratitude. Here we were, this eclectic group of people of different birthplaces, different professions, different ages, and different life stages. Surely we'd never have entered one another's lives if not for our mailing addresses.

G. K. Chesterton said, "We make our friends; we make our enemies; but God makes our next-door neighbors."[2] He claimed that Scripture speaks "not of one's duty towards humanity, but one's duty towards one's neighbour. . . . We have to love our neighbour because he's there."[3]

Jesus must have meant what he said about neighbors after all. How could I have thought it was possible to love an abstract neighbor Samaritan-style if I didn't love the people who lived next door to me? And it shouldn't have come as such a shock, but this neighbor business wasn't just a one-way deal. These people were neighbors to me, too.

As Blanca was leaving my house the night of her baby shower, she gave me a customary Latin kiss on each cheek. "I may be far away from family, but I feel really loved right now." And I guess that's how it's supposed to be. After all, she was my neighbor.

It wasn't the kind of community I'd been looking for (i.e., a husband and a family of my own), but God, as usual, seemed to delight in surprising me.

The Theology of Huckleberry Pie

IF HOSPITALITY IS AN INHERITED GENE, I should have it. Whenever my family made the long road trip from Illinois to visit my mom's parents on the West Coast (Grandma and Grandpa Washington, we called them, after the state), the topic of conversation from about Wyoming on was what varieties of pies would be waiting for us on her blue-marble countertop.

We were never disappointed. After a long round of hugs and hellos, we kids would make a dash for the kitchen to find the faithful spread of pastries—pie made from fresh-picked huckleberries, pie made from straight-from-the-garden rhubarb, cherry pie with crisscrosses like only Grandma can make. No matter what time of day we arrived, we'd have a slice (or two) while the kitchen buzzed with a dozen conversations.

My mom is no slouch herself in the hostess department. She's one of those people who has two sets of china—and uses both. Her formal dining room isn't reserved for holidays or bridge club; it's a regular gathering place for family and friends and children. When she serves her trademark homemade pizza there and red sauce inevitably spills on the white carpet, she calmly sticks to one of her life mottoes: "People are more important than things."

As a child, I had my share of courses in hospitality school . . . making homemade donuts and cookies while standing on a chair in Grandma's kitchen, helping Mom set the table and make place cards for guests. I guess I always figured my life would look a lot like theirs when I grew up—dinner parties with friends, brunches after church, homemade cookies in the oven, and a houseful of kids to eat them.

But now that my twenties were fading, I was realizing just how different my life looked from both my mom's and my grandma's. By the time they were my age, Grandma had three kids, and Mom had two plus another on the way. They had full-time jobs, all right, but not the kind you get paid for. Their days were filled with neighborhood play groups, church activities, volunteering, and taking care of their homes and husbands and children. My days were consumed with a full-time career, and the only things I was responsible for keeping alive were my houseplants (with mixed results).

Without the perk of a wedding registry, my kitchen boasted a haphazard assortment of hand-me-down dishes, garage sale items, and my ex-roommate's Tupperware. Somewhere in the bowels of my cupboard there was probably a pie tin, but I could say with some certainty that it had never seen the likes of a homemade huckleberry pie.

And there was another hurdle beyond the dishes. Me.

Truth be told, face-to-face hospitality felt pretty intimidating. I may have been getting more comfortable allowing Blanca to see the dust bunnies in the corner of my living room, but it was pushing the bounds of vulnerability to let people taste my attempt at dinner. And perhaps most of all, to let them into a part of myself.

I tried to let the whole idea of being intentional about hospitality fade into the background. After all, life was different now than it had been when my grandma was a young homemaker. Most people my age went out to eat together instead of having dinner parties in their homes. Maybe hospitality was a relic of an era gone by, a throwback from the world of Elvis and poodle skirts.

I had a backlog of excuses to cover every day plus leap year, and I figured I could get over the disappointment of failing to carry on a generational trait. But I couldn't seem to shrug off the thread of hospitality in the Bible that kept haunting me.

As I paged through the Gospel accounts, I was astonished at how many times Jesus gave his important theological messages not from a pulpit or at the Temple or in the form of a scholarly tome, but at a supper table. Sure, there were occasions when he preached at religious venues or gave sermons to the masses, but a significant chunk of his ministry took place at intimate dinner settings, in the homes of friends.

He kicked off his first miracle at a wedding reception, he invited himself over for a meal at Zacchaeus's house, and he went to a dinner party with a bunch of Matthew's sketchy friends. Of all the things he was accused of, one of the most recurring complaints was the company he kept for dinner.

Even on Jesus' last night, when you might expect him to be ironing out some last-minute theological issues with his followers about eschatology or predestination vs. free will, he instead chose to have dinner with his friends. And even as they were eating, he reminded them that this Last Supper wasn't really the end—that there would be an eternal dinner party to look forward to someday.[1]

Of all the visuals of heaven Jesus could have painted, he chose the intimacy of a communal table. And so I decided to begin gathering friends around my table too. I started small. At first I invited only safe people—people I knew would say yes and would love me even if the main dish was inedible and we had to order Chinese takeout. Then I worked my way up to inviting one safe person and one wild card. That way I could expand my dinner table (and my comfort zone) but still have the security of a buffer. Sometimes the food was mediocre; sometimes my planning was off and each dish was ready at a different time; every time the recipe didn't look like the beautiful photo I was using for reference.

But even so, amid all the imperfection and bumbling around, there was something sacred about inviting people into my home for a meal. I'm not sure I could precisely pinpoint the connection that took place as we passed haphazard-looking lasagna and lingered over dessert and coffee, but I had a hunch those interactions just might have been every bit as spiritual as reading a commentary or spending extra time in prayer. In some mysterious way, the dinner table served as a catalyst for an everyday miracle, a tangible expression of grace.

That's not to say it suddenly became easy. I still had plenty of excuses whispering in my ear:

I'm too busy. Too tired.
My house is a disaster.
My cooking skills are lackluster at best.
Would anyone really want to come?
What would we talk about?

But ultimately it wasn't really about the food and the flatware settings. It was more about the spiritual transactions that occurred within this shared space of a common meal. I hoped the people who crossed the threshold of my home would experience a taste of Christ before they left: a word of encouragement, a listening grace, the warmth of acceptance. Maybe even an attempt, however bumbling, at unconditional love.

Whenever my rationalizations crept in, I'd remind myself that my role model in this hospitality gig wasn't Martha Stewart. It was Jesus. If a thirtysomething bachelor with no fine china and no dining room could live a life of hospitality, I figured I had no more excuses. I'd have to do the best I could with what I had during this season, even if it looked different from what I'd imagined. And even if it meant I'd have to break out a store-bought pie for dessert.

Mole Checkups and Other Forms of Accountability

"THIS WILL ONLY STING for a little while," Dr. A. assured me as she picked up a rather ominous-looking pair of oversized clippers. I instructed myself not to look as she hacked off a mole on my rib cage and then stitched me up. I tried to fix my eyes on the family photo on Dr. A.'s desk, but a morbid fascination kept drawing my eyes back, train-wreck style, to her sewing. I couldn't help but wonder if she quilted in her spare time.

I hadn't expected such drama for the afternoon—not the immediate removal of the offensive mole or the doctor's decision to send that little piece of me off to the lab for more tests. Surprisingly, however, the worst part of the visit was still to come.

As I sat shivering in that awful tissue-paper excuse for a gown, Dr. A. glanced at my chart, frowning. "I'll call you with the lab results," she said. "But in the meantime, you need to have your husband check you regularly to make sure none of your moles have changed. Especially the ones you can't see." During the pause when she scribbled notes on my chart, I pondered why on earth I'd spent an inordinate chunk of my life filling out forms and checking the "single" box if no one bothered to read them.

"Uh, I'm not married," I said.

Barely pausing from her note-taking, Dr. A. said, "Oh, well, your boyfriend then." I tugged the white tissue paper gown closer around my middle. The most I could muster was a shake of my head. I could picture the personal ad now: "SWF looking for long walks on the beach and someone to check her back for iffy moles."

One of those *hmm?* noises exited through Dr. A.'s nose, and all at once I felt like my skin blemish was the least of my abnormalities. I think her mouth kept moving, but by that point I was trying to figure out how quickly I could get back into my clothes and hightail it out of there. This woman knew how to handle skin cancer, but apparently whatever I had was another story.

On the way home I was vaguely aware of a radio interview about the World War II–era German theologian Dietrich Bonhoeffer. Under other circumstances I might have switched to something that required the firing of fewer brain neurons, but I was too busy replaying the preceding conversation in my head to do anything about it. The irony that I was more concerned about my condition of singleness than my potential skin cancer (which thankfully I did not have) was not lost on me.

As I started tuning in to the spiel on Bonhoeffer's life, they zeroed in on two of his favorite topics—community and accountability. He believed it was impossible to have a healthy, growing faith without the context of close relationships—the kind that went beyond the superficial bounds of handshaking time at church. And apparently these weren't just theories for him; they were principles he lived out in the Bruderhaus ("Brothers' House"), when he was the head of the seminary there. Bonhoeffer had written *Life Together* out of this firsthand experience of living what he called "a genuine experiment in communal living."[1]

In his book Bonhoeffer offers the following warning about loner Christians: "Let him who is not in community beware of being alone. Into the community you were called—the call was not meant for you alone; in the community of the called you bear your cross, you struggle, you pray. . . . If you scorn the fellowship of brethren, you reject the call of Jesus Christ."[2]

His words are much more eloquent than mine, but my layman's interpretation went something like this: We all need someone to check our moles—the physical ones and the spiritual ones.

It was almost the New Year, so I figured now was as good a time as any to inaugurate a mole-checking campaign. But where, oh where, to begin?

I'd always been in awe of people who manage to pull off New Year's resolutions. Well, I suppose I had no trouble making them; it was just keeping them that got dicey. Maybe part of my issue is that I tend to make a list of the top sixty-nine goals required to achieve the perfect me, and I just can't sustain that kind of multitasking for 365 consecutive days.

So as a concession to my inability to keep resolutions past Groundhog Day, I'd made a habit of choosing a single theme for the year. The shorter the better. (At the very least, the brevity helped ensure that I wouldn't forget it.) One year it was "Simplify." Another time I picked "Give thanks." Then there was "Choose joy" and "Face your fears." The idea was to focus on one thing all year and really dig into what it would look like to, for example, simplify my closets, my time commitments, my junk drawer, my technology, the foods I ate, the constant multitasking in my brain. I'd run everything through the grid of the theme for the year and see what changes I needed to make.

As I thought about all the "moles" that could be lurking in my blind spots, I sensed that my theme for the year was choosing me: *Be accountable.* Forget the year of the ox or the tiger or whatever. This would be the year of accountability. I wanted to invite people to speak truth into my life—to ask them to show me my blind spots and help me see areas where I wasn't being the person I was made to be and not living the life I'd been called to live.

The hyperventilating started almost immediately after I spoke the theme aloud. What was I getting myself into? On second thought, maybe it would be easier to train for a triathlon, forsake all carbs, and stop smoking. (Not that I smoked, but you get the point.)

Even within the church, we have a tendency to elevate privacy over accountability. We do the obligatory greetings on Sunday mornings—maybe share a health- or travel-related prayer request or two at small group—but that's about the extent of it. Then we go back home and close our doors and stay out of one another's business, like good Americans.

Now that I lived alone, I didn't have a built-in person to call me on my stupid stuff. Which, I suppose, was all the more reason I needed it.

So I crafted a note to a handful of my closest friends and family members, posing to them the following questions and concluding with the promise that no matter what they said, I would hear them out and not get mad.

> *What am I doing that I shouldn't be doing?*
> *What am I not doing that I should be doing?*

A number of people didn't engage with the invitation at all—it's just as risky, I suppose, to dish out an honest critique as it is to receive one. But some of my friends did respond, and sure enough, I was blindsided by some of the things I got called out for. (Right. I guess that's why they're called blind spots.)

My sister, Meghan, was one of the brave souls to take me up on my offer. As I opened her e-mail with the subject line "The Year of Accountability," my hands were so clammy I could barely maneuver the mouse.

Oh boy, I thought, *what kind of payback will be in store for me after years of forcing Meghan to play pretend-school with me and heaven knows what other forms of older-sister torture?*

A hundred possible responses raced through my head, but there was no way I could have prepared myself for what I read:

> I feel like you're kind of . . . I don't know if this is the right way to say it, but . . . putting your life on hold. Like you're waiting to really start living until you get married.

Well. Nothing like getting knocked to the ground by a sisterly two-by-four.

I talked back to the computer, trying to poke holes in her claim. *Hey, I bought my own place, thank you very much,* I told the screen with as much snark as I could muster. *And I have a real job—a career, even—that I love. I have friends and . . .* But my protests were losing steam fast. Meghan was right, and I knew it.

I looked around the room at my eclectic furniture—hand-me-downs from kind aunts and uncles and grandparents. Those pieces did the job, and I was grateful. But it certainly wasn't what you might call grown-up furniture. The more I thought about it, the more I realized that the problem wasn't the furniture itself; it was my perspective—that this was all temporary somehow.

I thought about the file folder I had labeled "Travel," jammed with articles and pictures of the places I wanted to go someday—about

90 percent of them somewhere in Italy. *Someday*, I'd always thought, barely admitting what that actually meant: "Not till I have a husband to share it with."

I thought about my church—how the music soaked into a place deep in my soul, how the teaching made Scripture more real to me somehow, how I felt a tingle down my spine whenever the benediction was said. But I hadn't really started leaving my toothbrush there, so to speak. If the church is the body of Christ, then I was the self-appointed appendix. I hung around in the general vicinity, but no one really knew why I was there, and they could have functioned just fine without me. At some subconscious level, I guess I just assumed I'd be braver when I had a sidekick. *Someday.*

And perhaps the most significant aspect of Meghan's challenge pointed to something that wasn't tangible—something about my way of looking at the world. Somewhere along the way I read Jesus' words about abundant life and decided there was an asterisk by them—that real life wouldn't kick in until I had a signed piece of paper declaring me officially hitched. Which is even more ridiculous when you consider that the source of those words wasn't married himself.

But how could I get unstuck?

Thankfully my sister didn't do an accountability hit-and-run. She stayed around for the aftermath, and eventually we came up with a plan: Both of us would try one new thing every week. It didn't have to be big—just something we'd never done before. Then we'd report back by the next Monday about our escapade from the previous week. *Only one thing a week*, I thought. *Piece of cake.*

As it turned out, I was more of a creature of habit than I'd realized. Each week I had to be vigilant in my search for something new so I wouldn't find myself in a desperate situation come Sunday evening and have to resort to something ridiculous like trying to learn to crochet on YouTube. (Hypothetically speaking, of course.)

Some weeks were admittedly more stellar than others. But all things considered, it wasn't too bad for a girl who parked in the same row every time she went to Target. There was the week I discovered a new route to work, the week I checked out a new bike path, the week I had a short fling with Sudoku, the week I went out of my way to make a new friend, the week I slept on the other side of the bed, the week I joined a Sunday school class at church, the week I took up learning a new language, the week I added a new color to my wardrobe.

Then there were the less ambitious weeks when I had to confess to my sister (after hearing that her highlight was something like pole vaulting into a swimming pool) that I'd lamely tried a new brand of coffee or discovered a new blog. Sigh. I suppose sampling English Toffee half-caff is daring in its own way.

But during those weeks, I was learning a few things. (Well, except maybe when it came to Sudoku. Who was I kidding, trying to do something that smacked of math?) I was discovering that some of my routines and preferences weren't as necessary as I thought they were. Others were good and wholly me—but now I was starting to be more intentional about *choosing* those things, not just defaulting to them by habit.

And I was realizing how much my settling had to do with fear. Fear that things would change. Fear that things would never change. Fear that I would never find real and lasting love. Fear of failing epically. Fear of failing moderately and landing smack-dab in the middle of mediocrity. Fear of stepping out of what was comfortable. Fear of putting myself out there . . . and then being rejected.

But here's the secret about living, really living: You can't embrace life if you don't dance at the edge of your fears. If I kept trying to play it safe, I'd give my fears the power to call the shots, and I wouldn't be ready to embrace the adventures and the abundant life God had in store for me.

As the year came to a close, having attempted fifty-two new things, I felt bittersweet about turning the page on the calendar. It was a relief to have completed the experiment, and I was already contemplating something easier for the year ahead, like The Year of Sitting My Butt on the Couch. But I didn't want to give up on this idea of living fully, of embracing life. So I borrowed a prayer I'd read by the fourth-century desert father Sarapion of Thmuis: "We entreat you, make us truly alive."[3]

Yes, Lord. Make me truly alive. Iffy moles and all.

Where Would God Put His Tattoo?

A FRIEND OF MINE had just gotten a tattoo, and a group of us girls were sitting in a corner booth at a restaurant on a Friday evening discussing it.

"What kind of tattoo would you get?" my friend asked us. Everyone shared their options, but I found myself stymied. As I sifted through various possibilities, I realized the chances of my getting one were slipping from slim to nil.

Not because of the physical bravery of it all (although the thought of a needle on my skin did make me a bit woozy). Not out of fear that someday I might not want to draw attention to that particular part of my body (there was always the ankle option, after all). And not because of any lingering social stigma or religious conviction, either. When it came down to it, I guess the thing that impressed me most about people with the guts to get a tattoo was the permanence of the decision.

Think about it: Maybe you really liked Mickey Mouse back then . . . but after a few years you outgrew your Disney phase. Or maybe the peace sign was all the rage at the time . . . but you're not so sure you still want one on your shoulder a few decades later. Or maybe you were in love with Billy or Johnny or Tom when you got inked . . . but, well, what if things just didn't work out?

I thought about my friend Angela, who used to have a tattoo with Jon's name on it. It was a modest-sized tattoo, and she was pretty proud of it. Until she broke up with Jon, that is. Then she was faced with a decision: Should she go through the painful, expensive, and not-guaranteed removal process? Or should she get another tattoo to cover it up?

Angela opted for the latter, and after several attempts, Jon's name was covered by successively larger and darker tattoos until finally she was left with a fist-sized black flower that stretched across her abdomen. Angela confided to me that even worse than the physical pain was the tattoo's nagging reminder of the rubble of that broken relationship.

Not long after our tattoo conversation, I was reading the book of Isaiah, and these words hit me in a new way: "See, I have engraved you on the palms of my hands" (49:16, NIV).

In my years of following God, I'd bought into the concept of a reciprocal relationship with him. If you'd pressed me on the doctrine, I would have assured you that of course God's love is unconditional. But I lived as if I believed that if I obeyed him, if I did the right thing, if I was a good Christian girl, then he'd respond with love. If not, well, then, all bets were off. He was probably standing up there in heaven with his hands on his hips and a scowl on his face.

But this passage stopped me in my tracks. God had a tattoo. And it had *my* name on it.

This strange life stage of being unmarried and unattached as everyone around me settled into lifelong relationships was forcing me to look at some gaping holes inside me. For starters, how deeply I desired proof that I was loved.

I'd known since third-grade Sunday school that God so loved the world, but in the past few months, I'd been feeling bereft of evidence that he so loved *me*. Without tangible reminders like flowers or love notes or diamond jewelry, I found myself desperate for something to hold on to as affirmation that I was valuable, special, chosen. That I was worthy of love.

And as the ground of my relationships shifted under the weight of my friends' new life stages, I was realizing how much I yearned for something permanent. Even the closest of human relationships, I was discovering, were conditional, impermanent. Circumstances change, people don't stay the same, and geography gets in the way.

I longed for someone who would never leave me, never move away, never get too busy for me, never get tired of me. Someone who would never stop loving me. And in my more rational moments, I knew that this hole couldn't be filled up all the way by any friend, no matter how loyal; or by any man, no matter how much he loved me.

But a divine tattoo—now that was another story.

How could there be any greater proof of love than having my name tattooed on the hand of the one who loved me?

I was awed by the permanence of such an act. It spoke to a kind of commitment without conditions, a love that was offered with no strings attached. If I did something wrong or didn't live up to the ideal Christian-girl image, God wasn't going to scrape off my name or cover it up. His tattoo was proof that he loved me enough to go through the pain of having his palm pricked. And he loved me enough to make a public statement about it, putting it right there on his flesh, for all the world to see.

I was starting to get the point about God's love, but something about it was still nagging at me. "God, that's nice about your tattoo and all," I told him. "But it still feels pretty intangible to me." I couldn't see it with my eyes. I couldn't put my hand in his. I couldn't hear his voice telling me that things were going to be okay. I couldn't feel his arms around me when I felt alone. It would be nice to have someone with skin on. (Translation: *I'd like a husband. And could you get on that right away?*)

~∞~

As usual, God answered my prayer for affirmation that I was loved. But also as usual, the answer came in a different form than I expected.

One evening I was eating dinner with some friends and their four-year-old son. Among his many endearing qualities, Zach's claim to fame was being able to sing along with just about every "Weird Al" Yankovic song ever recorded. But his mom had taught him some good table manners too, so he politely sat through the boring "grown-up talk" during dinner. He seized the first lull in the conversation to tug on my sleeve. "I have a secret to tell you," he said.

I leaned down and he "whispered" into my ear, loud enough for the whole table to hear, "I love you!" I could have melted into my chair.

I was delighted to be the one on the receiving end of his secrets. Zach and I had been buddies ever since he was born. In fact, his mom had told me that before I'd arrived that evening, Zach had said to her in all earnestness, "I've been wondering about something. Is Stephanie my friend or your friend?"

About five minutes later, another tug, another whisper. This time: "I love you *very* much!" Throughout the evening, Zach's eyes lit up every time he thought of another way to express his "I love you" message.

As for me, my heart grew two sizes each time the secret was delivered, even though it wasn't much of a secret in the first place.

When I dug deeper into the Isaiah passage, I discovered that I wasn't the first one in need of a reminder of God's love. Thousands of years ago, God had assured the Israelites of the coming Redeemer and of his plan to save them. But the Israelites weren't convinced. True, they'd seen God's faithfulness in the past, but they were desperate for a reminder, for a little proof. They lamented, "The LORD has deserted us; the Lord has forgotten us" (Isaiah 49:14).

His response? "I have engraved you on the palms of my hands."

At the time Isaiah recorded these words, pagan worshipers were known for carving the name of their god into their hands. The throbbing pain served as a constant reminder of their devotion and left them hoping it would be enough to get the god's attention. It was into this mixed-up religious climate that God spoke . . . and turned things completely upside down. Instead of asking us to prove our love and worship, he took great pain on himself to show *his* love. And instead of demanding blood and sacrifice from us, he sent his Son to be the sacrifice in our place.

With full knowledge of what he was getting himself into, God made a decision to love his people. And not just the mass of humanity, either, but each of us, individually. He loved *me*, ugly parts and all. There was nothing temporary about it—his love wouldn't stop if someone better came along. And it wasn't based on what I could contribute to the relationship. It was a forever sort of commitment, a "not even death can part us" vow.

I still felt lonely sometimes. But I knew I wasn't alone. I had a community surrounding me—people who would try my new recipes, hold me accountable, and maybe even check my moles for me. And if I ever doubted God's love, his tattoo settled it now and forever. I belonged to him. Permanently. Unconditionally.

PART 4

Hope

He who hopes in God trusts God, whom
he never sees, to bring him to the possession
of things that are beyond imagination.

THOMAS MERTON, *No Man Is an Island*

Mr. Very

❀

A BUNCH OF US were at a company-sponsored picnic and minor league baseball game when my friend's roommate launched into an energetic commercial for the book she was reading. It was by a well-known author and psychologist in the genre I like to call Shameless Mate-Snagging, and the premise was simple: If you're having trouble getting a date, you're just not putting yourself out there enough.

The book provided suggestions about how to do more effective "opposite-sex networking" and how every woman should make it her goal to give her number to at least ten people a week (directly or through fellow networkers). The author even offered a money-back guarantee if you read the entire book and followed all his guidelines and still didn't have a date.

As a third-generation cynic about money-back guarantees, I found myself balking at his concept (although for the sake of full disclosure,

I must admit that I later forked over ten bucks to buy the book). Then the ball-game infomercial turned a corner from theoretical to personal.

"So, get this," she said. "One of the chapters is about how you should share your 'people resources' with each other. We all know single guys we don't necessarily want to date ourselves, but they might be Mr. Right for someone else." Her volume was increasing along with her enthusiasm, and I started glancing around to see who was overhearing this embarrassing discussion, trying to make sure my boss or other coworkers weren't in close enough proximity to take in our conversation.

Finally I realized she was awaiting a response from me.

"What name can you give me?" she repeated.

Umm . . .

"I'll give you the name of a guy I know," she repeated, "and you can do the same for me."

"Uh, no, that's okay." I was growing increasingly fidgety now that it looked like names would be traded around like baseball cards. "I really don't know anyone who would be right for you anyway."

She assured me it didn't matter. Apparently, according to Dr. Matchmaker's book, it was all about quantity. Better odds, I guess.

I remained resolute until the seventh-inning stretch, when, whether out of a sense of morbid curiosity or because I'd run out of excuses, I caved in to her repeated requests.

"Okay," I relented. "I'll talk to a guy I know and see if I can give him your number."

After the requisite squeals subsided, she conferred with her roommate and decided on the guy she'd contact for me.

And so it was that a couple of weeks later I found myself in the coffee area of a bookstore with a guy whose name really was an adverb, but I'll call him Mr. Very.

It didn't help that from the moment the little bell on the door jingled and he walked in, he was trying to impress me—not with the man he was, but with the man he wanted to be.

"I'm usually very prompt," he said. "I just had to take care of a few extra things for the dog today."

"I don't have very much money saved up yet, but believe me, someday I'm going to be very well off."

"I know I'm not in very good shape right now, but I'm going to join a gym and lose forty pounds in the next three months."

So many adverbs, so little time.

We made some small talk, and he filled me in about the dog he wanted to get someday, the upper-body workouts he had planned for later that week, and how his current job was just a training ground for what he really wanted to do. It's funny, I might have liked the actual Mr. Very, but I was having a hard time getting to know the real him.

It wasn't until I was headed home that a thought occurred to me: He had told me a lot about himself, but had he asked anything about me? I racked my brain, but I couldn't recall a single statement of his that had ended with a question mark.

Another blind date, another rock added to the Ebenezer pile. Apparently this wasn't going to be in the divine quick-fix category.

It was probably just as well. I had a lot to learn about hope. And I had a *very* long way to go myself.

(But was it too late to get my money back for that book?)

God and the Odds

"So, how's your love life?"

As I sat there in the vinyl reclining chair at the dentist's office, with my mouth propped wide open, I wasn't sure if it was the worst possible moment to be asked such a question or the best. Not that anytime would have been particularly convenient, seeing as the most accurate answer would have been something like, "Think about *Sex and the City*. Now picture the opposite of that, and you'll have it just about right."

My hygienist had known me practically since I had teeth, and she knew my whole family too, so I guess she felt a little more liberty with me than with her other patients. Still, as I sat captive in that chair, the scraping of metal in my mouth suddenly seemed like the least of the day's pokings and proddings. I made a mental note to see if relational interrogation violated some kind of HIPAA law.

While the hygienist did her work, I mumbled something semi-incoherent: "Ah mmmphh bmmph mmm uhmm." Which, roughly translated, meant something like, "I've gone on a few blind dates that didn't exactly go anywhere, but I'm sure the right guy will come along soon." Mental note number two: *Make sure I have something more substantial to report six months hence. Or at a minimum, aim for a cavity so at least we'll be able to land on another topic of conversation.*

Later that week I was minding my own business, reading an article in a magazine, when I was accosted by a terrifying stat: According to a demographic study done by the Barna Group, there are 13 million more Christian women in the United States than there are Christian men.[1] That's right, *13 million.* I mean, I was prepared to wait until I found a guy who was one in a million, but this was taking things a bit far.

Somehow, in this particular situation, it *wasn't* comforting to know I was in good company. What had seemed like a personal molehill of a problem suddenly felt like an entire mountain range. And as hopeless as that made me feel for myself, I was also miffed on behalf of all those other women who were doing numerical battle alongside me.

I was going to have to revise my answer at my next dental visit: "I've given up hope. There are roughly 13 million other women in my shoes, and we're all fighting over the same single Christian guy. Don't try too hard whitening my teeth—I don't stand a chance." But of course, with my mouth propped open, it would all just sound like Charlie Brown mumble anyhow.

My statistical freak-out sent me on a quest to find out if God had anything to say about numbers. Not being a numbers girl myself, I'd never given much thought to whether God liked math, but I started noticing that the Bible actually makes a pretty big deal about quantifying some of the details in Scripture. It's like God is flashing some kind of neon sign, calling our attention to the numerical parts of his story.

In some cases, I suspected the numbers were included for historical purposes—they offer credibility and context for biblical accounts. Cases in point: the number of days it rained while Noah and the rest of his crew were on their ark cruise (40); the number of years Methuselah lived (969); the number of feet Nehemiah and others repaired on one key section of the wall in Jerusalem (1,500); the number of people, including Paul, who were shipwrecked near Malta (276).

But in other cases, I wondered if the numbers were there more for spiritual purposes than for fact-checking reasons. Was it because God knows about our messy relationship with integers and how easily we humans can become slaves to numbers and statistics? With little warning, we can find ourselves consumed by them: the number on the bathroom scale, the number on our bank statement, the numbers on the blood pressure reading, the number of candles on our next birthday cake.

How was it that a couple of numbers had a way of utterly decentering my emotional equilibrium? Maybe that's why God emphasizes a new kind of math.

Take Gideon, for example. He lived in a time when the Israelites were clearly the underdogs. Fierce attacks by the Midianites had them cowering in caves, and the whole nation was basically on the brink of starvation. Enter Gideon. He seemed to be an average sort of guy, with his share of questions and doubts, but God called him to lead an uprising against the Midianites anyway. Gideon finally agreed and rounded up his military recruits: a whopping 32,000 soldiers.

But God's response at that point is startling—especially for someone like me who finds consolation in the strength-in-numbers mentality. Instead of congratulating Gideon on his impressive recruiting skills, he told Gideon, "You have too many warriors with you." So, in the face of the enemy's massive army, which apparently looked like "a swarm of locusts," God told Gideon to systematically reduce the size of his troops. The number of Israelite soldiers dwindled from 32,000 to 10,000, and then from 10,000 to 300. Only then did God say it was time to go to battle.[2]

The numbers were impossibly stacked against the Israelites . . . but that seems to have been the point. That way when victory came, they couldn't claim they'd done it on their own strength—they'd have no choice but to acknowledge God's hand in beating all human odds.

So I had a choice about what I was going to put my faith in: statistics or the God who brought victory to an against-all-odds army. Would I trust my own strength or the God who also brought Sarah a son when she was ninety years old, the God who added 3,000 people to the church in a single day in the book of Acts, the God who rose from the dead after three days? If he was big enough for those kinds of miraculous numbers, maybe he was big enough to handle the scary numbers in my life too.

I also realized that just because God *could* overcome those alarming numbers in my life offered no guarantee that he would. But it was grounding to remember that the numbers that threatened me and consumed me were no match for God. In fact, he had quite a track record of laughing in the face of the most daunting odds.

Maybe that's what those numbers were all about, after all: not mere historical markers, but quantifiable reminders that God isn't scared by statistics. That he can't be reduced to a formula. And best of all, that he is greater than any number I could have thrown at me.

That's my kind of math.

A couple of weeks later, I saw I'd missed a call from my dentist's office. *Weird,* I thought. *They don't usually contact me unless they're reminding me about an upcoming appointment.*

I heard the cheerful voice of my hygienist on the message. "I just had the most *wonderful* idea," she gushed. Apparently she had another patient who was *just perfect* for me—he was tall and handsome, came from a good family, and best of all, had *great teeth*.

"Your kids would have such beautiful smiles!"

And then she started rattling off his phone number, HIPAA notwithstanding.

I never could bring myself to make the call. I wasn't sure if this unsuspecting fellow even knew he'd been dragged into a setup, let alone that the status of his future children's pearly whites had been a topic of conversation. And I shuddered to think about what kinds of questions my hygienist would ask about my love life if I were with a guy she actually knew.

Even in the face of bad odds, I would still choose hope. Wherever God would lead me on this journey, I figured this waiting and wondering might at least scrape some of the plaque off my heart.

The Red Couch

WHEN JESUS TALKED about the abundant life in John 10:10, I'm pretty sure he was primarily referring to deeper issues like salvation and eternal life, not twenty-first-century home furnishings (carpenter though he was). But I was banking on the fact that he makes concessions for the likes of shallow folks like me and allows us to get a glimpse of something big and spiritual and otherworldly through things that are rather ignoble on their own. Like, for example, my couch.

Although my year of trying new things was over, I couldn't stop thinking about what my sister had said about putting my life on hold. I looked at the couch in my living room—my companion for so many years—and suddenly it struck me as symbolic of all the ways I'd been pausing my life.

The couch and I had found each other through an unusual set of circumstances. My uncle, who always has an eye out for treasure, had happened on the couch on the curb of a neighbor's property. After confirming with the owner that it had merely sustained a little water damage but was otherwise in good shape and free for the taking, Uncle Bob secured it for me and transported the hefty thing to my first apartment. It had served me well over the years, and with the help of a few strategically placed pillows, no one even noticed the water stains.

But now, I decided, it was time to get a grown-up couch. Not so much for the feng shui of the room or to meet some unspoken set of interior decorating standards, but as a symbol that I wanted to really embrace my right-now life. Not my someday-when-I-have-a-husband life. And so I started stashing away money for the couch fund and studying furniture store ads as if they were literary masterpieces.

Mom and I went shopping together, and I kept looking at all the practical options—pieces that wouldn't get dated quickly, neutral colors that would blend with my current decor. But then I saw it. The red couch. I made a beeline toward it, wondering if love at first sight was possible after all. But it was when I sat in the matching red chair and accompanying ottoman, with all its potential to become the Reading Chair, that I knew for certain we were meant to be.

When the salesclerk was finalizing the sale, she asked if I wanted to start with a down payment or pay in full. Having saved diligently, I pulled out my checkbook, feeling a surge of satisfaction that I wouldn't be going into debt for my purchase. The woman handed me my receipt and circled the date I could expect the furniture to arrive at my house. I grinned. That would give me four weeks to consider paint colors.

Two weeks later I received a voice mail from an unknown number. I almost deleted the message when the prerecorded voice came on, but something made me pause. "We regret to inform you that our company has declared Chapter 11 bankruptcy," the robotic voice intoned. "None of our stores nationwide will remain open." Apparently they had no intention of giving me my red furniture . . . *or* returning my money. So much for being fiscally responsible and paying for everything up front.

After the requisite internal ranting at the soon-to-be-defunct furniture company, the lousy economy, and myself for attaching so much significance to a fabric-covered spot to plant my rear end, I played the single-girl card I reserved for such desperate situations. I called my dad.

He was just as riled as I was, but he wasn't just going to rant about it; he was ready to take action. And so we made a plan: My job would be to find stores in the same chain that had floor models of each piece I'd purchased. He'd take care of making sure that they let us take the furniture home with us.

The next day I got a list of each of the chain's stores in the Midwest. After scores of phone calls, I finally found all three pieces I'd paid for: the red couch, the red chair, and the ottoman. There were just two caveats: (1) Each piece was at a different store . . . within a five-hour radius of each other, and (2) the stores claimed they were not authorized to fulfill orders with floor displays.

Yeah, well, they hadn't met my dad.

One Friday Dad and I embarked on our quest, armed with only his pickup truck, my receipt that read "Paid in full," and a touch of vigilante justice.

We arrived at the first store, the one with the ottoman.

"This will be the critical stop," Dad told me. "If we can get this one, we can get them all." He told me his plan had two phases, if necessary. Strategy number one would be Mr. Nice Guy; strategy two would be Papa Grizzly Bear.

Fortunately, we never had to resort to the second strategy. Dad had the manager so razzle-dazzled that he was about ready to throw in a coffee table on the house.

After leaving the building to pull Dad's truck around, I tried my best to hold back my victory dance until we were safely out of sight. Dad drove to the loading area and started backing his pickup down the icy ramp that read "Shipping Trucks."

"Uh, Dad?" I hated to put a damper on the celebratory moment, but something didn't seem quite right. "Do you think this is the ramp for the *big* trucks . . . you know, like the delivery vehicles? No offense to your Chevy."

I eyed the steep, ice-coated ramp nervously as we continued backing down. But Dad remained undeterred. "Nah, this is it."

After waiting a while at the shipping area with no ottoman in sight, we finally spotted another loading area—this one for "civilians" like us. Just one problem: There was no way the truck was going to make it back up the icy hill.

Dad spun his tires for some time without success, and then he looked at me. "Do you want to drive or push?"

Gulp.

Neither option seemed quite like my forte. But I'd never driven a stick shift, so I figured my only real option was to push. In retrospect, I do recall Dad saying something about not standing behind the truck, but how else are you supposed to push a large vehicle up a hill? Especially if you're a girly, bookish type whose arm curls are limited to picking up her purse?

People usually say such moments happen in slow motion, but in this particular case it all transpired so quickly I barely had time to realize what was happening. As the truck slid backward and pinned me against the brick wall of the shipping building, I had only one pathetic thought running through my head on constant repeat: *I'm going to have an ottoman and no legs! An ottoman! And NO LEGS!*

After some creative shimmying, a few bruises, and eight hours of traipsing around the state, Dad and I returned to my place exhausted but with all three pieces of furniture—and with all appendages intact. I'd never been so grateful to have someplace to sit down as I did that night. And the nicks on my floor-display furniture only added to the charm—scars of sorts to remind me of all I had to be grateful for.

I have to say, that night as I sat in my brand-new, hard-won chair, I felt life running through my veins. Maybe even in abundance.

UnValentine's Day

MY RED FURNITURE was secured and arranged in place just in time for Valentine's Day. That would have seemed auspicious, had I been the type to celebrate the holiday. But in fact, I wasn't. At least not anymore.

How, I wondered, had this day that once brought so much childhood delight in the form of decorated shoeboxes and pasty candy hearts deteriorated into the Black Day of Despair?

Every February I spent the better part of the month doing acrobatic maneuvers to dodge romantic Valentine's Day commercials in all their forms. Then, come February 14, I'd hunker down at home with only a chick flick and my bowl of mac and cheese for company.

But this year I wanted things to be different. Perhaps I was bolstered by the recent red couch victory, or maybe I just wanted to show off my newly coordinated living room. In any case, I decided

I wasn't going to let Cupid—he of the apparent bad aim when it came to me—win this year. So I sent out invitations to the single women I knew—a girl in college, a woman who'd recently been widowed, an acquaintance who had just broken up with her boyfriend, and some friends who for unknown reasons weren't getting roses from suitors this year.

We would have an UnValentine's party, I decided. Not Anti-Valentine's, just UnValentine's. No mourning, no man-bashing, no wearing black. Just a girls' night. And most important, we'd have a theme: chocolate. Strawberries in chocolate fondue, decadent chocolate-frosted cupcakes, gooey chocolate truffles, Ghirardelli hot chocolate—you name it.

A couple of days before the party, I was feeling pretty good. The cupcakes were in the oven; the vacuum was out, if not on; and I'd picked out what I was going to wear (blue seemed like an appropriate "un" color). That's when a thought punched me in the gut. From past experience, I knew that kind of a delivery usually means it's either a nudge from God or the result of eating something expired (those little stamped dates on food packages are merely suggestions, right?). But this time the thought wouldn't go away: *Invite Cheryl.*

I wish I were a better person and could tell you that I immediately picked up the phone. But there was a lot more, well, dialogue than that. I gave God the top forty-nine or so reasons why it wasn't such a good idea for me to invite Cheryl. Yes, she was my friend, and she had that contagious joy that always made me smile. And while, in my reckoning, her Down syndrome was just one of the things that made her Cheryl, along with her devotion to her cat, Frisky, her obsession with singer Bebo Norman, and her ability to recall facts from any given story in the Bible, I was just a little self-conscious about what my other friends would think.

In her thirties, Cheryl lived at home with her parents and had a childlike heart and a pure faith that I admired and consistently learned from. But even so, I wasn't sure how she would fit in a social setting like this one. Would Cheryl monopolize my time as she tended to do when we hung out together? Would she give hugs to unsuspecting guests and make them feel awkward? Maybe I could do something with her another time, just the two of us. I tried to convince myself it had been the week-old beef and broccoli.

But the nagging feeling wouldn't go away, so I finally grabbed my phone.

On the other end of the line, Cheryl squealed with delight before I could even get out all the pertinent information. "This is just wonderful!" she exclaimed.

How could I have questioned the nudge?

The next day I got a call from Cheryl's mom while Cheryl was at her piano lesson. "You have no idea what an answer to prayer this is," she told me.

I tried to lodge a protest, mentally replaying my grudging obedience.

But she pressed on. "One morning last week Cheryl came to me and said, 'Oh, Mom, something wonderful is going to happen this Valentine's Day. I just know it!'" She was a little concerned about how much stock Cheryl was putting into this unfounded dream, and although she didn't want to squash her daughter's childlike faith, she felt she needed to temper her enthusiasm somehow to protect her from getting hurt. But each time she tried to speak a little realism into the situation, Cheryl just grinned and confidently reiterated that "something wonderful" was going to happen.

I gulped, realizing how close I'd come to missing out. I had no doubt God would have made some other wonderful thing happen for Cheryl. But I'd come awfully close to not being part of it.

When Cheryl arrived at the party, she was decked out all in red, from her red-sequined shoes to her red headband and red heart-shaped earrings. I needn't have worried about her monopolizing my time—she was way too busy making eleven new friends. And yes, she did hug a bunch of people, but by that time they were no longer strangers; they were her friends. And come to think of it, that's probably the perfect thing to do on UnValentine's Day.

After everyone left, there was a trail of chocolate fondue right in the middle of my new couch. But to my surprise, even that didn't put a damper on my joy. I'd lived in freeze-frame long enough to know that you can live your life preventing spills, but it gets pretty boring. When you live life on full, chances are it's bound to overflow past the edge sometimes. You've got to embrace the messy as a side effect of the abundance.

And I could console myself with this, at least: Even if I'd paid for the stain warranty on the couch, it wouldn't have done me any good anyway.

Baby-Step Prayers

To an outside observer, our weekly small group probably looked awfully messy. We preferred to call it eclectic.

We didn't fit the usual small group mold—we went to different churches, we weren't all the same age, we were in different life stages. But as it turned out, that was a good thing. Maybe we weren't all going through the same struggles, but it was refreshing for me to get out of my mopings about my manless state and care about someone else's problems for a while.

Over the past several years, in addition to going through several Bible studies together, our group had walked with Heather and Rick through the hard road of infertility. We'd grieved with them as they faced one setback after another . . . as the latest medical intervention didn't work, as they faced another heartbreaking miscarriage, as they woke up each morning daring to hope again.

The sting of it all was that I couldn't imagine a better couple to raise a little person. They had so much to give—a warm, welcoming home with an empty room just begging to become a nursery, the means to care for a child, a solid relationship, and most of all, a lot of love for a baby they'd never even met.

Week after week we prayed for God to intervene as he'd done countless times throughout Scripture—for Sarah, for Hannah, for Elizabeth. But months passed, and we got no answer. Then one week, after much waiting and praying, Heather and Rick told us they felt God was calling them to adopt. We all rejoiced with them, eager for what this new adventure would hold.

After carefully filling out form after form of what Heather referred to as their "paper pregnancy," going through a battery of interviews and tests, and writing an extensive profile complete with photos and essays, Heather and Rick figured the only thing left to do was wait.

They just never imagined they'd be waiting so long.

One birth mother agreed to have them adopt her unborn daughter, but near the end of her pregnancy, she decided she wanted siblings for the baby and went with another adoptive family instead. Another pregnant woman chose them but changed her mind and decided to raise her child on her own.

But then there was Krissy. She was a good kid from a good home who'd made some choices she regretted when she went away to college. She knew she couldn't raise a child at this point in her life, but she wanted to find someone who would take good care of her baby.

She was smitten when she saw Heather and Rick's profile—she noted their warm smiles and cheered herself with the thought that her baby would be raised in the company of a fluffy white dog named Newton. And she couldn't hide her excitement when she noted that both she and Heather had strawberry blonde hair. Who knows— maybe her baby would even look a little like her adoptive mom.

And so they agreed that when it was time for the baby to be born, Heather and Rick would fly out and meet Krissy and sign the paperwork to make it official. They lived several states away, so even more paperwork was required, but these hoops seemed like nothing compared to the joy awaiting them. After years of waiting, this was finally happening. As they counted down the days, Heather thought she even felt some sympathy pangs of morning sickness.

Meanwhile, Lent was just around the corner, and I wanted to do something to mark the season. I just wasn't sure what. The church I attended didn't do much to observe the church calendar, but this discipline felt like something tangible I could do to ground my faith, to gain some spiritual equilibrium. In the past few years I'd given up something I loved (coffee, sweets, chocolate, even crossword puzzles) with the idea that those small sacrifices might prompt me to contemplate Christ's infinitely more significant sacrifice. But nothing was striking me as the right thing this year.

Then one morning it hit me: This Lent, instead of taking something away, I'd add something.

But first, I'd need some supplies.

I went to my favorite paper store and bought the prettiest spiral-bound journal I could find. On each of the forty days of Lent, I decided, I'd write out a prayer for Krissy and the baby, asking for God's protection and guidance over this whole process. By the time Easter rolled around, the baby would be well into the second trimester, and by my estimation, thoroughly swaddled in prayer.

The process started out a little on the awkward side—I hadn't written out prayers much before, and on top of that, it was strange to pray for someone I'd never met. But gradually it became more natural, and before long I was on a roll, praying for this tiny baby's physical development, future calling, relationships, and spiritual journey. I asked God to give this child a strong sense of identity and value, and for a healthy relationship between Krissy and Heather and

Rick. I asked God to redeem this situation for Krissy somehow. And I praised God for this miracle, this answer to so many prayers.

Just after Easter, Heather and I got together for lunch. I hadn't told her about the Lent experiment yet, and my plan was to give her the journal full of prayers that day. I pictured her sharing it with her child someday when he or she was old enough to understand, and I tried to imagine how that child would feel knowing that his or her life was covered in prayer even before birth.

But as we sat there spooning out creamy sweet potato soup at one of our favorite restaurants, Heather seemed a little down, and I decided to wait until the right moment to hand over the journal. But as the meal progressed, the right opportunity never seemed to come. Then, as we were getting ready to pay the bill, Heather took a breath.

"Stephanie, I need to tell you something." Her words hung in the air. "Krissy miscarried."

I knew I should say something to try to comfort her. But all I could do was look down at the notebook in my hands. The leather cover was trembling. Finally I managed to look at Heather. And I cried. I cried for Heather and Rick. I cried for Krissy. I cried for this baby. I cried for the unfairness of it all. I cried for the shattering of yet another hope.

And I cried because my prayers—all forty days of them—had miscarried too.

Feathers and Axes

ALL THAT SPRING I found myself in something of a tiff with God. I had some choice words for him, asking what kind of Father would take the hopes of this mom- and dad-to-be and dash them against the rocks. My heart was broken for my friends. And to be honest, I was asking the question for myself, too.

This desire I'd been longing for—to love and be loved, to have a family of my own—it wasn't a bad thing. It wasn't like I was asking him for wads of illicit cash or a string of one-night stands or a syringe full of heroin. I reminded God that Heather and I were asking for good things—things *he* invented, by the way. Just in case he'd forgotten.

It didn't help that engagement as a diagnosed condition was practically contagious all around me, but I seemed to be immune. At work we celebrated the fifth engagement in the span of four months—in my department alone. This brought with it the usual sideshows: showers; gifts for said showers; and incessant talk about wedding registries, cake tastings, and honeymoon destinations. Not to mention the sense of dread I felt with each invitation that arrived. Would this be another event I'd have to attend without a plus-one? There are only so many times you can go to the restroom during the dancing before you become way too conspicuous.

When we gathered in a coworker's office to hear the story about the latest engagement, the newly minted fiancée said with a laugh, "Okay, maybe we'll have a break from engagements for a while now!" I looked around the room, and sure enough, every woman there had a diamond solitaire except me. *God, how can I keep doing this? How can I keep trying to rejoice with those who rejoice when my own hopes continue to dismantle into heaps of rubble and disappointment?*

I wondered—again—if there was any point to hoping. If you don't hope for something and God delivers, it's a pleasant surprise, right? And if you have no expectations and that longed-for thing doesn't happen, well, then, maybe it prevents a little piece of your heart from breaking.

It had been a while since I'd seen my mentor, Ruth, and I felt bad about it. We'd originally planned to get together once a month or so, but several months had gone by since my last visit. The truth was, I wasn't sure I wanted her to see me in such a spiritual funk. Based on previous experience, I knew she had access to some kind of truth serum that made everything leak out of me when we were together, so it wasn't like I could just try to get together for a cup of tea while chatting about fluffy topics like the weather and which prince of England was more dashing.

Eventually my excuses ran out, though, and I made the phone call, deciding my tactic would be to ask so many questions that there wouldn't be time for me to spill how ticked I was with God. And at the very least, I'd be on the receiving end of a fantastic breakfast.

"Tell me about Brazil," I prompted over my piping hot cup of coffee.

"Hmm." Ruth looked out the window, where a slender willow tree waved its branches in the courtyard. So different, I thought, from the lush jungle foliage of Brazil, where she and Bob had spent a decade early in their marriage.

"Did I ever tell you about the time Bob died?" she asked me.

Before I could blurt out something obvious about how I knew for sure he was alive and well in the basement at this very moment, Ruth went on. "Well, he didn't actually die. It's just that everyone else thought he did."

Ruth passed the tray of homemade breads—cinnamon streusel and zucchini chocolate chip—and I settled back in her big striped chair to hear the story.

She and Bob had left South Dakota for Brazil several years before. They were catching on to the language by then, making connections with the people in the village and finding opportunities to share about God's faithfulness and grace. Ruth and Bob had three children by that point, two of whom had been born in Brazil without the luxury of modern hospitals and the medical advances they would have had access to back home.

But despite how different the farming community where they'd grown up was from their new home, with its anacondas, poison dart frogs, and malaria, Brazil was starting to feel like home—even if they were six thousand miles away from their families. Bob always said that Ruth had a special gift for making a home no matter where they found themselves, even in the middle of the jungle. No matter that their hut had a dirt floor that Ruth swept clean each morning or that bugs swarmed in through the cracks in the walls each night or that the kitchen stove was little more than a pot over an open fire.

One morning Bob left early to go into the nearest town—a three-day journey through treacherous ravines and over rough mud trails.

Ruth kissed him good-bye while the children were still asleep and began the morning chores.

A week after he was due to return, when Bob still wasn't back, she started wondering where he might be. She knew by now that jungle time operated on a different clock than the Western world did, and it wasn't uncommon for plans to get delayed. But Bob wouldn't want her to worry, and he did everything he could to keep his word.

After two weeks passed, people in the village started to approach Ruth with pronouncements of doom. They told her they were sorry, but her husband was probably dead. After all, the street bandits had a tendency to target foreigners.

"But he didn't have any money on him," Ruth protested.

"No matter," they said. "To the highway robbers, all white men are rich."

Three weeks after Bob was due to come home, someone from the mission board paid Ruth a visit. "It's time to pack your things and head home," he said. "The jungle is no place for a widow and her children." Then putting his hand on her arm, he said, "Ruth, I'm sorry. Your husband isn't coming home."

But Ruth remained undeterred.

"I can't explain it," she told me, "but God gave me this deep assurance that Bob was alive. I wasn't going to give up hope."

Hope. There it was—just the sore subject that had been at the root of my rift with God. How could Ruth have known?

"But how did you keep on hoping when it looked impossible?" I asked. "Even when it seemed crazy to keep holding on?"

Ruth just shrugged. "Hope wasn't something I manufactured on my own. It was something God planted there."

"So what happened? When did Bob come home?"

Ruth smiled. "One afternoon, more than three weeks after he was due to return, I was in the kitchen preparing supper, and from down the dirt road, I heard whistling."

"Whistling!" I exclaimed. Pastor Bob was famous for his whistling.

Singing wasn't exactly his forte, but name any tune, and he could whistle it. I remembered how easy it was to find him at church—you simply followed the cheerful canary sounds.

"Yes, it was Bob all right. It turned out he had sent a telegram telling me that he was detained and that he'd be back late, but the message never made it to me."

Ruth paused to offer seconds of the bread to me. "You know, I wonder if hope is a different journey for each person. It doesn't seem like the hopers in the Bible had a formula for it."

I wanted a faster solution, a faith-drip that would instantly pump Ruth's brand of hope into my own veins. But it looked like I was out of luck for a shortcut.

As I looked through the Bible over the next few weeks, trying to find these "hopers" Ruth mentioned, I found company in my wrestlings from a rather obscure story. I read the account of the woman from Shunem in 2 Kings and discovered that despite the thousands of years and a significant cultural gap between us, we were sisters.

According to the story, this woman and her husband had shown hospitality to the prophet Elisha when he was in town, and he wanted to do something for her in return for her kindness. She insisted that she didn't need anything—she had a pretty good life already. But Elisha heard that she had no children, and he immediately proposed the perfect gift for her: "Elisha said to her as she stood in the doorway, 'Next year at this time you will be holding a son in your arms!'" But her immediate response wasn't as overflowing with joy as you might expect: "'No, my lord!' she cried. 'O man of God, don't deceive me and get my hopes up like that'" (2 Kings 4:15-16).

Sure enough, though, she had a son, just as Elisha had promised. The miracle came true. Her hopes were fulfilled. But that's not the end of the story.

When the boy was older, he was working out in the field with his father, and all at once he became ill and died. The Shunemite woman went straight to Elisha, and she had a few words for him. "Did I ask you for a son, my lord? And didn't I say, 'Don't deceive me and get my hopes up'?" (2 Kings 4:28).

I'd never had a son, and I had no clue where Shunem was. But I had a hunch this woman and I would get along just fine. I knew what it was like to get my hopes up, only to have them shattered on the rocks of real life. I knew what it was like to long for a man's hand on the small of my back, to have someone look at me like the rest of the world no longer existed, to have someone to dream with about the future, to have a man who would whisper in my ear that he wanted me to be the mother of his children one day. I'd hoped silently and furiously for those things, but I couldn't see anything moving even remotely in that direction.

And I didn't have an answer to my predicament: Was there any compelling reason to hope? I thought about Emily Dickinson's famous poem that describes hope as "the thing with feathers/That perches in the soul."[1] That was about the level of gravity I attributed to hope when I overheard myself talking about it: "I hope it won't rain." "I hope he'll call me." "I hope that semi coming toward me gets back on its side of the road." Like Emily, I treated hope like so much wishful thinking, a feather that fell haphazardly wherever it chose.

After doing a little more digging about hope, I was intrigued to discover that in church history, the image used to depict the idea was pretty much the opposite of a feather: an anchor. Up until around the fifth century AD, the anchor was one of the main symbols for Christianity, more prevalent than a cross. Believers in the first century even had the image of an anchor etched into their tombs as a symbol of the eternal hope they clung to.

Maybe that was the problem, I thought. All along I'd been thinking of hope as a feather, when the more appropriate metaphor was an anchor.

What if hope wasn't so much about the thing I was hoping for itself but a tether to keep me close to God, the granter of hopes? Without hope, I'd drift aimlessly in the big ocean of doubt and fear and uncertainty. Hope was a good thing, but only when it was anchored in a person, not a circumstance.

As it turned out, the woman from Shunem did get her son back after he was miraculously brought back to life. Heather and Rick had no such guarantee about whether they'd get their longed-for miracle, and neither did I—not about whether I'd find a husband in the first place or whether I'd get to hang on to him for a while once I found him. But whatever God decided to do with the desire of my heart, I decided I wasn't quite ready to give up on hope. I had to believe that hope would pull me back, closer to the heart of the one who anchored my soul.

No offense to Emily Dickinson, but maybe it was time for me to adopt a weightier analogy. Writer Rebecca Solnit offers her own equally weighty metaphor: "Hope is not like a lottery ticket you can sit on the sofa and clutch, feeling lucky. . . . Hope is an ax you break down doors with in an emergency."[2]

From now on, I wanted hope to look less like wishful thinking and more like this: bringing my big prayers—along with my big disappointments—to God.

It was time to bring out the ax.

PART 5

Prayer

*It is when things go wrong, when the good things
do not happen, when our prayers seem to have been
lost, that God is most present. We do not need the
sheltering wings when things go smoothly. We are
closest to God in the darkness, stumbling along blindly.*

MADELEINE L'ENGLE

The Linebacker

THE LINEBACKER WAS the kind of guy who could make you go weak in the knees when he merely looked at you. With his intense blue eyes, his wavy blond hair, and an upper body sculpted like an upside-down pyramid, all the females where we worked (married or otherwise) were prone to swoon whenever he walked in the room.

But as for me, I wasn't about to fall for such shallow nonsense. I knew the jock type: high on ego and brawn, low on brains and depth. Not that it really mattered, of course, since guys like that were never interested in bookish types like me.

What my foolproof jock-protection system failed to take into account was this: What if one of those types *did* show interest in someone like me?

I suppose it wasn't technically a setup with The Linebacker since we'd already met, but the coworker who played matchmaker just kind of moved things along. With her salt-and-pepper hair and multi-colored reading glasses, Mary was the mom of the department, always bringing in homemade bread, recommending her favorite books, and making sure the younger employees were taking care of themselves and not working too late.

One day when she saw The Linebacker and me chatting in the hallway, she told him, "You know, you should take her to dinner." (I should mention here that nobody really said no to Mary, so I'm not sure he had much of a choice.)

Shortly after our mutual friend suggested we get together, I dropped my flash drive in the break room, where several coworkers had gathered, including The Linebacker. Before I could pick it up, he swooped down and grabbed it. But instead of handing it back to me, as I'd expected, he put it in his shirt pocket and headed back to his office.

And in that moment, despite my flaming cheeks and the gawking cluster of coworkers, a fatal chink fell out of my anti-football-player armor.

Not long afterward I was working late, standing at the copier with my back to the door. Suddenly I heard a deep voice behind me.

"What's a cute girl like you doing working so late?" he asked. "Let's get out of here and get some dinner," he said.

My heart started pounding so loudly I was sure he could hear it. I turned around, and all the rules I'd heard about not going out with a guy unless he gave you at least three days' notice flew instantaneously out of my head.

"Um, okay?" Nothing like this had ever happened when I was on this side of the movie screen, and I'm not sure if I agreed out of the sheer surprise of it all or because I was so flattered by the attention of someone who could have walked out of a movie himself.

As we drove separate cars to the restaurant, I quickly applied some lip gloss, wishing I'd worn a sassier outfit to work. There was something niggling in the back of my mind that maybe I'd have known to dress for a date if I'd been asked properly, but I shoved the thought aside, reveling in the fact that a guy—a *cute* guy—had asked me out. *Besides*, I figured, *this is just the first time he asked me. I'm sure he'll plan ahead in the future.* Then I checked myself. *If he asks me out again,* I reminded myself sternly.

As it turned out, he did ask me out again. But the pattern remained much the same. The invitations were always spontaneous offers for the same day, and the tone was casual: "Hey, if you're not doing anything later . . ." or "I feel like getting a bite to eat . . ." He always paid, and he always made charming comments that indicated he was interested. I kept telling myself that he wasn't disrespecting me; he just wasn't a planner. But the strange thing was, he only invited me out on Monday through Thursday, and his social calendar on the weekends always seemed to be filled with engagements I wasn't privy to.

As The Linebacker and I started getting to know each other, it quickly became apparent that while he was into the idea of being a Christian up to a certain point, he wasn't too interested in anything that required a real lifestyle adjustment. He didn't see a discrepancy between partying until he passed out on a Saturday night and then dragging himself to church the next morning.

I didn't join him on his binges, and I thought he'd grow tired of hanging out with a Goody Two-Shoes. I was becoming more and more convinced that this wasn't going to work, but every time I looked into those eyes, I lost my resolve.

Ironically, I got the courage to end things when he gave me a compliment.

We were sitting in my office, and I told him it seemed like there were just too many areas we didn't see eye to eye on.

"No, we balance each other out," he claimed.

I was trying valiantly to avoid eye contact. Argh, those baby blues.

"You can be the spiritual one in our relationship," he continued. "We'll be a team."

That's when he put his hand on my knee, just at the hem of my skirt.

Electric currents were making their way to all extremities except my brain. I was rapidly losing resolve.

Then he said it: "You're perfect."

All at once the spell was broken.

In that moment I had what I can only describe as a vision of one version of the future, as if God were lifting the curtain of time and letting me see what The Linebacker's life might look like in several decades if nothing changed. What I saw was a paunchy, middle-aged man pounding back the brewskis in front of the TV, expecting his wife to toe the moral line on his behalf. I knew those were good-girl shoes I'd never be able to fill.

Shakily, I slid off my chair.

Twenty years from now, those blue eyes just wouldn't be enough.

"No." My voice was quavery but resolute. "I'm not perfect. Not even close."

Breaking Up with Church

IT HAPPENED ONE SUNDAY MORNING at the eleven o'clock service.

I wasn't done with God, but doggone it, sometimes the church just *hurt my feelings*. I knew it wasn't right to base a long-term relational decision on one event while forgetting all the good my significant other had done in the past. But then again, breaking up isn't always completely rational.

My church was (finally) wrapping up a sermon series on marriage. As hard as it had been to go week after week and hear about God's beautiful design for marriage and the way God said it isn't good for man to be alone, I dutifully went and took notes, telling myself that hopefully this would apply to me someday and I'd be the better for the background knowledge. Or at least maybe it would help me support my friends in their marriages.

But on the final Sunday of the series, the pastor had a rock-star idea for how to wrap up the service.

"Everyone, take five minutes to pray with your spouse," he instructed. "Right here, right now, just pray where you're sitting."

I eyed the nearest exit. *Is it too obvious if I have a sudden urge to head to the ladies' room at this precise moment?* But I realized I'd chosen my seat unwisely, and I'd have to crawl over several cozily praying couples to get to the aisle. I'd just have to stick it out.

I wish I could say I bowed my head and prayed for all the marriages represented in that room, as a more mature friend I talked to after the service had done. Instead, I sat there coaching myself through those agonizing five minutes, vacillating between *Don't bolt, Don't cry,* and *Don't break any of the Ten Commandments on church grounds.*

I'd had a special connection with church ever since I was a kid, and I couldn't imagine my life without it. Granted, my church experience as a single woman in a relatively large church scarcely resembled my childhood experiences, and to some extent, that was my own fault.

Despite my year of accountability, I knew that at some level I was still holding back, waiting to really dig in until I could introduce myself as part of a couple, until I could plug in with a husband and children one day. And truthfully, the church hadn't quite figured out what to do with people like me. I didn't fit in with the college group, I didn't fit in with the young marrieds' class, and I didn't fit in with the moms' group. Although I tried to cobble together community where I could, I mostly floated around in ecclesiastical limbo. But as I allowed my mind to drift amid the low hum of praying voices all around me, I realized that up until that day, I'd never felt like I wanted to leave.

❧

When I was growing up, I saw church as an extended family of sorts— a place where I was known and accepted by a wide net of adults beyond my parents. It was a place where Mavis would ask me about school and Lila would pray for me and Rosie would give me beautiful hair bows she'd made so I could accessorize my '80s side ponytail.

Mom served on practically every committee and volunteered to help just about anytime the doors were open. By default, that meant we kids were signed up too, and I have memories of vacuuming between the pews, putting the little Communion cups in the trays, and setting up chairs for potlucks.

And let me tell you, that church knew how to do potlucks. A significant portion of the church was made up of old-school Scandinavians, meaning every major occasion warranted an impressive spread of food to be set out after the service. You could guarantee there would be a strong showing of Jell-O salads, some kind of meatball dish, and best of all, an entire table devoted to dozens of assorted desserts. What the Scandinavians may have lacked in exotic entrées, they more than made up for with their pies and layered-pudding deliciousness.

I remember one Sunday when lunch was being served to thank a group of volunteers who had put together a big church event. It was February—one of those cold, blustery days Chicago specializes in. The smell of meatballs and cheesy potato casserole must have wafted up the stairs and out into the cold afternoon air, because shortly after we sat down to eat, a homeless woman made her way to the church basement in search of a hot meal.

Everyone stared at her for a moment, and then in a flash my mom was out of her seat. She exchanged introductions with the woman and then took her by the elbow, ushering her toward the huge spread of food.

Back at the tables full of church ladies, the murmuring started.

"She shouldn't be here," someone whispered.

"This food is meant only for the volunteers," another said, looking pointedly at my mother.

Someone else piped up, a bit more diplomatically but just as emphatically, "She might feel out of place here."

With all my twelve-year-old idealism, I was indignant. Partly because I'd heard the Sunday school lesson about the goats and the sheep and had been schooled about Jesus' words: "Whatever you did not do for the least of these, you did not do for me" (Matthew 25:45, NIV). Perhaps most of all, I was outraged because it was *my* mom whose judgment they were questioning.

The moment the woman sat down at our table (causing a few people to excuse themselves to use the restroom, only to return to a different table), my moral high ground wavered. *Would Jesus have made an exception in the case of severe body odor?*

On the way home I expressed my outrage to Mom. "Why weren't they going to let her join us?" I asked.

Mom was more charitable. "They weren't trying to be mean," she said. "They just didn't know what to do with someone who's so different from them. They didn't understand her."

I came out of my little reverie and looked around at all the couples bowing their heads together and either holding hands or putting their arms around each other. As I watched them pray and recalled the earnestness in the pastor's voice, I heard Mom's voice echoing in my head. These people weren't trying to be mean. They just didn't know what to do with me.

And how, I wondered, would they ever understand if I bailed when I got in a huff about something? You can't break up with someone without having the decency to at least try to bumble through the reasons. And although I certainly didn't see myself as the Che Guevara of the single population, maybe I could speak up on behalf of this rather invisible segment of the church. At the very least, I could stick around to serve as a reminder that not everyone who follows Christ files taxes jointly and drives a minivan.

On Monday I composed an e-mail to the pastor. After a slew of revisions, I finally struck what I hoped was a cordial tone. (In the end I decided against the more belligerent subject line "Please stop the persecution of the singles among us!") I thanked the pastor for his commitment to strong marriages and then asked him to consider the unmarried contingent of his congregation if he did something similar in the future—not just for my sake, but also for those who had lost spouses through separation, divorce, or death, or for those whose spouses didn't attend church with them.

I checked my e-mail with one eye shut for a couple of days, wondering how—or if—the pastor would respond. Finally a message appeared in my in-box. "Thanks for the feedback," he wrote. He told me that he'd considered preaching about singleness, but it "affected such a small number of people." I resisted the urge to respond with a snarky comment that unless every couple in the church died simultaneously in their sleep or met their demise in car crashes on the way home from date nights, singleness would, indeed, affect all of us at some point.

What would my gracious mom say? I wondered.

Then I read the e-mail stamp at the bottom of the pastor's message. Under his name was the following blurb: "Join us for the next exciting sermon series on Ephesians 6: Raising Your Children God's Way!"

I sighed. Church and I were in this for the long haul. But clearly this was going to be one of those rough patches in our relationship.

Fighting My Dragons Alone

❀

THE SUMMER OF WEDDINGS was well in my rearview mirror by now, and I took this to mean life would settle down and there wouldn't be so many changes for a while.

I was wrong.

The ground was shifting under my feet again—just for different reasons this time. The Anti-Loneliness Campaign list, with its names of people I could call at any time of day or night, was still on my fridge, but it had gotten buried behind Chinese takeout menus and Christmas card photos. I knew those people would still be there for me, but they'd all entered new phases of life. They had husbands and babies, new responsibilities and different priorities—and rightly so.

The small group that had been my lifeline disintegrated in practically a fortnight. Two friends moved to Texas. Another moved to Florida. The rest of my small group was absorbed by a church I didn't attend. My neighbors Blanca and Rodrigo moved out of state after he got transferred for his job. I was finding it much harder to be brave about inviting people over when I didn't have a core of safe people I knew would show up.

"The problem is that I don't have a *person*," I lamented to Sarah one day that summer.

"A person?"

"You know, a daily person. The logical one to write down as an emergency contact. The one you call when you're in a crisis. The one you tell about the random funny thing that happened to you at work that isn't really worth calling someone about. The person you check in with at the end of each day and say good night to."

I found that I liked living alone, and despite my qualms about having to single-handedly kill all the spiders that ventured into my house, I was pretty independent. Still, there were moments when I felt vulnerable, both physically and emotionally. I was confident I could handle the ordinary, day-to-day challenges, but what would happen when something bigger and scarier than a spider came my way?

One typical Monday morning I went to my work mailbox and found an interoffice envelope with another envelope inside it, the smaller one clearly having been opened and resealed with tape several times, as if the sender had been second-guessing whether to send it.

My stomach went sour the moment I opened it. It was from one of my coworkers—a seasoned and respected man who I knew was married with several children. The note was filled with unsolicited praise for me . . . but not about my work. It gushed about my personality, my talents, my appearance. It didn't qualify as sexual harassment, but it felt completely out of line. It made me feel like I was getting dragged into something shameful and ugly. Yes, I wanted to be told I was beautiful—but not by a married man.

My first reaction was a mixture of horror and guilt. Had I done something to indicate that this kind of communication would be welcome? I was sure I'd done nothing to solicit attention like this. I felt angry, exposed, vulnerable.

And utterly alone. *Who's going to take my side?* My mind kept tripping over the question. Here was this man with lots of years under his belt and an impeccable reputation. I, on the other hand, was the new girl just starting to establish myself. And so I didn't tell anyone, feeling a vague sense of shame and guilt, even though I knew I hadn't done anything wrong.

The next day, my hands shaking and my heart racing, I confronted him in person. "Please don't ever contact me again," I said, delivering the line I'd practiced all evening in front of the mirror. I prayed he wouldn't be able to detect the quaver in my voice. He mutely nodded his assent.

I escaped to the restroom and leaned against the metal stall door, tears of relief springing to my eyes. *You did it*, I told myself. *It's over.*

But it wasn't—not really. Two weeks later, another letter appeared in my box. More gushing. More effusive compliments. *How dare he?*

I was angry at him for putting me in this spot. I was angry at myself for feeling so helpless. And I was angry at God for leaving me alone to face my dragons. *If I had a husband*, I told God, *surely this guy would never have had the guts to try such a thing.*

For the first time since I'd had to face the mean girls in middle school, I found myself waking every weekday with a pit of dread in my gut. No one had laid a hand on me, but I still felt violated somehow. This place that had once felt safe had now been robbed of its security. I panicked every time I had to go to the break room, the front office, or any other common area, and I changed my route as I walked the hallways. Waves of nausea accosted me every time I had to check my mailbox.

After a few weeks of this routine, I realized that best-case scenario, I was careening toward an ulcer. I knew this was unsustainable, but I didn't know what to do. It was probably a little late in the game to get a black belt in tae kwon do.

For the most part, I felt like I could handle life without a man. I supported myself financially, I owned my own home, I knew how to do some basic home and car repairs (and how to call Dad if the problem was out of my league). And between my family and a solid core of girlfriends, I had a decent support system.

But in this scenario, Olivia Newton-John was right: I needed a man. I told God as much—how it would be really handy if he'd just plop a strong, protective guy in my path who would defend me and help get me out of this ugly spot. And in case he was wondering, yesterday would have been better, but now would work out just fine.

From past experience, though, I'd gathered that God didn't typically work according to my timetable or proposed shortcuts, efficient and helpful as they might have been. So I picked up the phone and made three big calls: one to my parents and two to good friends who also happened to be married to good guys. Something about getting my story out and having multiple sets of strong shoulders to help distribute the weight was freeing in itself. But we also agreed some action needed to take place.

Thanks to their wise counsel, I decided against the martial arts idea and opted instead for a civil conversation with Human Resources. I was shaking like a November leaf as I set foot in the office, afraid that they wouldn't believe me or that they'd take his side. But there was something about knowing I had the support of six people who loved me that pumped courage into me with each thump of my hammering heart.

To my relief, HR backed me up, warning my coworker not to contact me again and promising action if there was another incident. And to his credit, the man apologized to me through the HR representative.[1] But even though the dragon was no longer at my heels, it was still in its lair. And as week after week passed, I wasn't feeling the peace I'd expected, even though no more unwanted envelopes appeared in my box. That's when I realized there was an even bigger dragon I needed to face: my own fear.

I knew the right answer, of course. I should pray about this. But for some reason, I just couldn't force out any words—not out loud, not even in my head. It was like fear had lodged itself somewhere around my middle and snaked its way up to my throat, smothering the words before they could hit the air.

It was in this season of choked silence that I heard about an ancient prayer technique called sentence prayers. Monks in the early centuries AD became well known for their prayers, but for the most part they weren't the verbose, articulate numbers I might have expected. Instead, their prayers were usually simple, repetitive sentences, often spoken while the monks were doing dishes or sweeping or doing other menial tasks for their community.

"There is no need at all to make long discourses," said the fourth-century Egyptian monk Macarius. "It is enough to stretch out one's hands and say, 'Lord, as you will, as you know, have mercy.' And if the conflict grows fiercer, say, 'Lord, help!' He knows very well what we need and he shows us his mercy."[2]

I liked the sound of that: no long discourses. Maybe, just maybe, I could pull that off.

And so, every time I had to walk down the hallway or enter a communal area, I whispered silently to God, over and over: *Hang on to me. Hang on to me.* I imagined Jesus standing beside me, gripping my hand, protecting me. My simple cry wasn't original to me; it was merely an echo of the psalmist's prayer generations before me: "Yet I still belong to you; you hold my right hand" (Psalm 73:23).

In the battle against my fear dragon, it didn't seem like much of a weapon, but it was all I had.

As time went on, there were days I'd wake up without that dreaded pit in my stomach. And on one landmark day, I even returned to my normal routes at work. My prayer life wasn't much better, but at least the fear was loosening its iron grip on my soul.

One day as I was walking down the stairs at my job, I felt God nudging me that it was time to take it to the next level.

Will you forgive him?

Give me a break! I wasn't thinking about forgiveness; I was looking for protection.

But I also knew that I didn't want to stay where I was, perpetually running on this spiritual hamster wheel. And the longer I kept this guy on the hook for what he'd done, the longer I'd stay stuck too.

And so the sentence prayers continued, but with a twist: Now my countless repetitions also included "I forgive him." The shift was so gradual I barely perceived it, but one day as I was praying, I noticed that my throat had loosened. I had words again. And perhaps most surprising of all, the prayers that came flooding out of me were for this man—not that he'd get zapped by lightning, but for his marriage, for his wife, for his children, for his walk with God. And I actually meant them.

Somewhere along the way, I realized I owed God an apology for lodging so many complaints about how he'd left me defenseless. He hadn't left me alone after all. He'd surrounded me with people who cared about me and protected me—family, friends, coworkers. And most of all, he'd been right there with me the whole time.

I didn't give you a knight to slay your dragons, he seemed to be telling me. *I gave you a whole army.*

The Sacred Scar

It had been an intense week, to be sure—and not just because of
the lumpy plastic hospital chair that had served as my bed for the
last couple of nights. On Monday, a surgeon had cut through Mom's
body, sawed out the deteriorated hip bone, and hammered in a new
one made of ceramic and metal. I'd heard about plenty of other people
who had gotten hip replacements, and the surgeon had assured me this
was a routine procedure. But when it was my mom on the operating
table, the one who was always there to comfort me when something
went wrong, suddenly there was nothing remotely routine about it.

Everyone assumed the procedure would be a textbook case since
Mom was in great shape and otherwise healthy. But from day one
post-op, we experienced one fiasco after another. First there was the
morphine, which sent Mom's body into convulsive, feverish episodes
every thirty minutes. Something about the drug didn't agree with her

system, and she became hallucinatory whenever it circulated through her body. Then, almost immediately after surgery, Mom sensed that something was wrong with her leg—not her hip, but her leg. She asked the doctors and nurses about it, but they all assured her this discomfort was standard.

Several days later, however, when the morphine had worn off enough for her to think rationally for ten consecutive minutes, she had my dad and me take a look at the leg that was bothering her. To our horror, we saw what amounted to a partial tourniquet on her leg. The compression socks—intended to be tight enough to prevent blood clots—had been put on wrong. Instead of being flush and smooth all the way up her leg, they had gotten bunched tightly around her skin. And now, wrapping all the way around her thigh, was a gaping wound.

Suddenly there was a flurry of activity around Mom's hospital bed, and with it multiple rounds of blame transfer. In addition to the problem of the wound itself, the doctors were concerned about the possibility of infection. If this cut didn't heal properly, any infection could go directly to the susceptible new incision . . . and she'd be back to square one, needing to have the hip replaced all over again.

Once that danger had passed and she was discharged from the hospital, I stayed with my parents for a week to help Mom with basic tasks like putting on her shoes, going up the stairs, and getting into bed. Oh, and putting antibiotic ointment on that wraparound laceration. Preferably without my passing out. One day as I was doing wound duty, Mom asked me how it looked. I went through the checklist given to me by the medical team: The skin didn't smell necrotic, was no longer oozing, and was turning a healthy pink. Check, check, and check.

Mom let out the oxygen she'd been holding in. *Things are starting to look up*, I thought.

Then she said, "No one's talking about this, but there's going to be a huge scar, isn't there?"

I inspected the ugly red mark winding its way around her left thigh. Then I looked straight at my mom—the synchronized swimmer with the fantastic legs, even as a grandma.

"Yes," I whispered. "I'm so sorry."

While Mom napped, I tried to focus on the work I'd brought along with me but kept coming back to my own scars. Not the physical ones, like the mark on my nose from the time I had a bad case of chicken pox or the one on my shin from that nasty fall off the balance beam, but those well-hidden scars on the inside. Most of them were healed over, but I couldn't help but run my fingers over them and acknowledge their presence, with their slightly jagged edges and rumpled exterior.

If I looked closely enough, I could find the demeaning remark my fourth grade teacher had made to me, the cutting words about me in the junior high "slam book," the blowup with a college friend that had severed our relationship. There was the scar of rejection from every guy I'd liked who didn't return the interest, the now-healing incision from the married man at work.

Some of the scars were deep; others barely scratched the surface. Some I could finally joke about; others would probably always be tender to the touch. I believed that God is the great Healer, that he can clean out and stitch up any wound, no matter how deep. But even after he brings healing, even after the miracle of forgiveness, the scars still remain.

The question was, what would I do with those scars? Would I relive the pain of the incision every time I ran my fingers over one of them? Would I hold on to my anger at the people who inflicted them . . . or the God who stood by and let them happen?

On my last day with Mom before I headed home, once she was more mobile and it looked like her wound was clear of infection, she looked up from the hospital papers she was sorting through. I was startled to see her eyes brimming with tears.

"Every time I see this scar from now on . . ." Her throat constricted, and my mind whirled over what she'd say once she found her voice again. Would the scar remind her of the nurse who'd put on the compression socks incorrectly? Or the doctor who'd failed to listen to her when she voiced her concerns? Or would each viewing of the scar trigger memories of the awful days in the hospital under the influence of the body- and mind-ravaging morphine?

I was floored when these words came out of her mouth instead: "Every time I see this scar, it will remind me of the way God took care of me."

I couldn't help but think about the Bible hero Jacob, who had some hip surgery of his own. Jacob's wrestling match with God (Genesis 32:22-32) left him with a wrenched hip, and he walked with a permanent limp from that day forward. No doubt his tweaked hip was a tangible reminder of his encounter with a God who doesn't usually show up so tangibly.

I wanted what my mom had, after all. Not a new hip, per se. (I hoped this condition wasn't genetically determined, as the surgeon implied.) But I did want her perspective on scars. That it isn't so much about what happened in the first place or who inflicted the wound. It's really about the one who healed it.

The Promise I Thought God Broke

I WAS SITTING in the first meeting to prep for my upcoming service trip when, without warning, I felt a swelling wave of panic rising inside. Who was I to think I had anything to offer—either to this team or to the people we were hoping to serve in Central America? My construction skills were limited to whatever could be remedied with duct tape, and my Spanish was limited to whatever was on the menu at Taco Bell. Imagine my sense of betrayal when I discovered that *chalupa* doesn't actually do anything for you south of the border.

As the team leader ran through the list of expectations for our trip, he mentioned that each member would be responsible for leading devotions on one of the evenings. I meant to get on that right away, I really did. But other items on my to-do list seemed to take priority, like planning games and activities for the kids we'd meet, learning how to say, "Chicken tamale, por favor," and finding a cute rain jacket.

After several days in Central America, our group had bonded over shared experiences: eating rice and beans for breakfast, waking up to find a gigantic spider on the wall just above our heads, facing near-electrocution in the shower (I was pretty sure OSHA had never seen the likes of those exposed wires).

But most of all, we'd gotten a glimpse of true hospitality as we visited the homes of local foster families. These people barely had room for their own children, yet they'd opened their living spaces and their hearts to kids who were orphaned or whose parents could no longer take care of them.

We saw the joy on little Lucia's face when she told us about being adopted by her new "forever family." We delighted in the chubby cheeks of a six-month-old who was once skin and bones but who, under the care of a gregarious pastor and his wife, soon earned herself the nickname Albóndiga. "Little meatball."

Perhaps the most eye-opening experience of the week happened on the last day, when we went to the slums to do some construction projects. As soon as we entered the neighborhood, I understood why it was called a *precario*. The homes, which consisted of little more than mud and scrap metal, were built precariously into the side of a hill, ready to slide into the murky water below as soon as rainy season hit. Children roamed around barefoot in raw sewage and scrounged through garbage for food. The single ray of sunshine in the community was the little church, where the kids were served peanut butter sandwiches for lunch (likely their only real meal of the day) and were taught songs, Bible stories, and arithmetic.

My group was charged with pouring a concrete floor for the home of a woman with eight children. I'm not sure exactly what I'd expected, but I certainly wasn't picturing that we'd have to shovel wheelbarrows full of dirt and debris out of her home before we could even get ready to pour the concrete.

By the time our team got back to the dorm that evening, I was exhausted. My arms ached from mixing cement all day, and my heart throbbed even more. As I collapsed onto my air mattress, I had a fleeting thought about the group devotions I was supposed to lead that night, but it was hard to focus as my eyelids grew more unwieldy by the minute.

All at once I woke to the announcement that it was time to circle up for devotions. I figured I could wing it since the Scripture passage and questions were outlined in our group workbook, but I thought I should at least get a general feel for what we'd be talking about. I skimmed the verses and questions outlined for us to discuss. My stomach heaved when I caught a glimpse of the key passage for the day.

Now I should clarify at this point that I believe all Scripture is inspired, and I'd never want to risk lightning bolts for claiming anything otherwise. But I have to say that some segments leave me baffled, frustrated, or downright unsettled. And some, well—some I just don't like very much. Unfortunately, Psalm 68:6 was one of those: "God places the lonely in families."

Sure, I appreciated the sentiment of the promise. And I did (at least in theory) believe that God keeps his promises. I just hadn't seen how that particular verse played out in my own life. Sure, I had great parents and siblings, but now that I was an adult, I lived alone, with neither the husband nor the children I had imagined I'd have one day.

As I made my way to our meeting place, I wrestled with a few questions: How on earth was I going to lead any kind of coherent discussion, what with the images running through my head of beautiful, barefoot, motherless children picking through garbage? And on a personal level, how could I make sense of it all in light of my ringless finger, my childless arms?

What was I supposed to do when confronted by a verse that kind of felt like an empty promise?

I took a breath and looked around the circle, thankful that the singing time allowed me to collect myself (and/or stall). I spotted Maggie, who may not have had the biggest muscles in the group but more than made up for it with her maternal instincts. Having been a foster mom herself, she was able to relate to the families we met in a way no one else could. Then there was James, who didn't say much but took in everything and was able to communicate the few words needed (in English or Spanish) to clear up any number of miscommunications. There was John, who wasn't exactly the touchy-feely type but could fix any broken thing in sight.

There was Dan, the leader of the group, who stayed up after everyone else was asleep one night to wash all our filthy shoes. There was Rachel, who spent the precious moments of free time we had writing notes of encouragement to each person in the group. There was Ruth, the artist, who had a tendency to butcher words in Spanish but managed to communicate seamlessly with the kids through crayons and the universal language of pictures. And of course, Lily and Otto, the parental figures of the group, who surreptitiously orchestrated four rounds of singing on my birthday, which just so happened to fall on the second day of the trip (it was sung twice in English and twice à la "Feliz Cumpleaños").

And suddenly it hit me: What we have right here, *this is family*. Not the family I had envisioned, perhaps, with the strong, sensitive husband; the two kids; the dog; the white picket fence. But family nonetheless.

If family means praying together to a common Father, sharing the same living space (even if it was a sketchy, spider-filled dorm for a week), covering for one another's weaknesses, then sure enough, this was family.

Shortly after that first revelation came a second: Not only had God given me this quirky family, but as we sat around on those sticky plastic chairs in the middle of Latin America, I wasn't lonely.

Maybe there was more to that psalm-promise than first met my eyes—and my heart—after all.

My Quest to Become Annoying

I PULLED OUT MY BAG of rocks and turned them over one by one. *Blond Date. The Professor. Uber-Fundamentalist Boy. Mr. Very. The Linebacker.* These rocks were supposed to remind me of God's faithfulness. And in some abstract way, I suppose they did. I had a fuzzy sense that God was working in this and that he had a plan for me, but it felt like seeing the yeti's footprints when you wanted to see the mysterious big guy himself.

As I sat on the floor of my bedroom, holding those rocks in my hand, I tried to pray. But I just couldn't seem to find the words anymore. I'd been praying about this one desire for so long, and it felt like one of four scenarios was happening: (1) maybe God wasn't listening; (2) maybe he couldn't do anything about it; (3) maybe he just didn't care; or (4) maybe he was saying no. Whatever the case—neglect, impotence, apathy, or withholding—I wasn't sure I wanted to keep asking, only to be met with such agonizing silence.

All at once a memory from the last evening of my service trip fluttered at the corners of my mind. God had shown me something about faith in the context of a pieced-together family that night. What if the principle still applied now that I was back home?

And then suddenly I felt these words make a crash landing somewhere in my soul: *You need a prayer buddy.*

Gulp.

That sounded great except for two key limiting factors: *How?* And *who?* Seriously, talk about a conversation killer: "Hey, God told me I need a prayer buddy. You win! By the way, I'm kind of in a prayer slump myself right now, and I tend to be rather awkward praying out loud. Wanna sign up?" Yeah, I was sure people would be lining up any moment.

I told God I'd give it a try—on one condition. He'd have to show me the exact person to approach. And it was a one-shot deal. I'd ask one person, and if that person said no, I was off the hook. (I should mention here that I do recognize the audacity of telling a sovereign God what to do. But God is often gracious about answering prayers, even from a brash asker like me.)

I guess it shouldn't have been such a shock when one day my coworker Mason and I were recounting the previous evening's episode of *The Office* and the conversation eventually turned to more serious matters. She'd recently heard a sermon about the annoying neighbor in Luke 11:

> Suppose you went to a friend's house at midnight, wanting to borrow three loaves of bread. You say to him, "A friend of mine has just arrived for a visit, and I have nothing for him to eat." And suppose he calls out from his bedroom, "Don't bother me. The door is locked for the night, and my

family and I are all in bed. I can't help you." But I tell you this—though he won't do it for friendship's sake, if you keep knocking long enough, he will get up and give you whatever you need because of your shameless persistence. (verses 5-8)

"Shameless persistence," Mason said. "What do you make of that? I mean, it sounds like such a rude model for prayer."

"I know," I concurred. "When the story starts out, you expect Jesus to say this is an illustration of how *not* to treat your friends."

In my world, you're supposed to ask politely for something, and then if you don't get what you ask for, you walk away and try to be content about it.

"Do you think this means God really wants us to pray annoyingly?" she wondered.

As I sat there in that stiff-backed chair in her office, I froze. It couldn't be a coincidence that I'd been told to look for a prayer buddy, and here we were, having this freakishly relevant conversation.

But I had an excuse list long enough to impress a truancy officer. For starters, Mason and I didn't know each other that well. I was sure she had other people she'd rather pray with. And besides, she'd no doubt think I was several shades of crazy if I asked her to be my prayer partner.

Yet this was undeniably what I'd asked God for. *Well, I'll just throw it out there*, I thought. *And then when she says no, I'll be off the hook.*

Before I could talk myself out of it, I blurted, "Hey, what would you think about getting together to pray once a week?"

I didn't dare look at her, equal parts of me pulling for a no and a yes. I think she surprised us both with the swiftness of her response: "Yeah, let's do it." Then she added, with a laugh, "Maybe we should make our motto for the year 'Be annoying.'"

And so every Tuesday during lunchtime, we started getting together to pray about the things that were going on in our lives and the desires of our hearts—including the big request of a husband for each of us. It felt clumsy at first. God had shown me *who* to pray with, but I was still clueless about *how*.

At first we spent the first part of the hour chitchatting, trying to avoid the prayer-elephant looming in the corner. We spent most of the rest of the time *talking* about what we were going to pray about. The actual prayer part got squeezed into the last few minutes, the words coming out as skittish as a newborn foal.

But we were praying. We certainly hadn't arrived at the annoying level yet, but with each Tuesday that passed, we were growing less timid. One of the lines from the *Book of Common Prayer* echoed in my mind during those lunch breaks: "God, you are always more ready to hear than we to pray, and to give more than we either desire or deserve."[1]

More often than not, our prayer points came out in the form of emotional spew, and our ramblings leading up to those requests sounded for all the world like senators pulling off a filibuster. To my relief, Mason wasn't a professional pray-er, and she didn't expect me to be one either. As our Tuesday meetings gradually melted into habit, I'm not sure our prayers got any less messy, but maybe we were getting more comfortable with the mess. And perhaps most surprising of all, I was learning that God wasn't necessarily looking for poise and polish either. Maybe he didn't mind so much when I put my prayers out there in their rawest form, trusting that he'd sort them out somewhere between my mouth and his ear.

And something else unexpected was happening along the way: Mason and I were forced to discover more about this God we were praying to. Was he a good Father or not? That answer would color everything.

As we prayed about an ever-increasing list of things, big and small, we started noticing some startlingly direct answers. Granted, things were as stuck as ever on the man front, but we couldn't deny these other divine interventions that were adding up to be more than mere coincidence.

Was God listening? Yep. Was he powerful enough to intervene? Check. But did he *care*? That was what we were still trying to figure out. Yes, we realized he had bigger issues on his plate than matchmaking, like nuclear weapons in North Korea or disappearing ice caps in the Arctic, but still, did he care about two of his daughters who, in a tiny office during their lunch break, were praying their hearts out that a good man would find each of them?

I read in Matthew 7:

> Keep on asking, and you will receive what you ask for. Keep on seeking, and you will find. Keep on knocking, and the door will be opened to you. For everyone who asks, receives. Everyone who seeks, finds. And to everyone who knocks, the door will be opened.
>
> You parents—if your children ask for a loaf of bread, do you give them a stone instead? Or if they ask for a fish, do you give them a snake? Of course not! So if you sinful people know how to give good gifts to your children, how much more will your heavenly Father give good gifts to those who ask him. (verses 7-11)

Did I really believe God was like that? Was I convinced that he would give me a lobster buffet, not a cobra?

In many ways my dad was old school when it came to raising us kids. He had high standards, and we were expected to work hard and pull our weight. He could be firm with us, giving us what he called "sensitivity training"—as in making us *less* sensitive. Most nights at dinner he'd try to toughen us up through spirited banter and debate, playing the role of devil's advocate so we'd be ready for the real world.

But I knew without a doubt that he loved me. He'd never give me a rock or a snake (unless it was a harmless garter snake, in which case he might conspire with my brother to wave it in front of my face, just to make me squeal).

My mind wandered back to a scene with the twelve-year-old me, when my family was on a cross-country trip to visit my grandparents. I was decked out in my favorite outfit, and in case you've forgotten, wardrobe and accessory coordination was not something to be taken lightly in the early '90s. I was sporting a black-and-white polka-dot shirt, black stirrup pants, polka-dot earrings, and a hair bow to match. Then there was the pièce de résistance of the outfit: my brand-new knockoff Keds in—you guessed it—black and white. I was sure of it: Those kids in Washington State had never seen anyone as cool as me.

But before we arrived at my grandparents' house, Dad spotted a sign for a state park just off the highway. It would do us good to get out of the car and stretch our legs for a bit, he declared, brushing off our protests that it was raining.

"Oh, you guys are babies. That's not rain—it's just mist."

And so we set out on a hiking trail, despite the ever-thickening "mist."

I flipped up the hood of my coat, hoping to salvage what was left of my mile-high, amply hair-sprayed bangs, and trudged on. But then we hit the bridge. At least I thought it was a bridge. It was hard to tell because at the moment it looked like one giant mudslide.

There was no way I was going to let my beautiful new shoes touch slop of that caliber.

"Can we head back?" I pleaded. "Or at least go another way?"

But one by one, my family members crossed the bridge ahead of me. I stood rooted to the spot, sure they'd turn back once they saw I was serious. *I will not budge*, I steamed silently, arms akimbo. But they didn't throw so much as a backward glance in my direction.

I had melodramatic visions of being found several days later by a forest ranger, having survived on grubs and rainwater, black-and-white shoes still more or less intact. But despite my efforts to be brave in the face of abandonment, I felt my eyes starting to sting, and I was pretty sure it wasn't the rain. I didn't want to be separated from my family, but there was no way I could change my mind now. I'd made my stand.

Then, through a curtain of tears and rain, I saw my dad heading back over the bridge. *Wait . . . why is he coming this way?* I wondered. Would I get a lecture? Would he tell me he was disappointed I was being a wimp?

But as he got closer, I saw the twinkle in his eye. "Hop on my back," he said, crouching down. I couldn't believe it. I was way too old to be getting piggyback rides. But the rest of my family was on the other side, waiting, and I couldn't see any other way. So my dad carried me across that muddy bridge, knockoff Keds and all.

I supposed if I was looking for a model of how a father responds to annoying persistence, this moment when my dad came to the rescue of a daughter whose outfit was in jeopardy was as good a model as any.

I looked at the passage from Luke again, and something struck me: Nowhere did it say that the father was compelled to give his child precisely what she asked for, that the child could special order what she wanted from a gift catalog. It just said a good father would give good gifts to his children. What if the gift God wanted to give me was different from the one I'd been asking for? What if the thing I thought was good was merely a snake dressed up as Mr. Right?

A good dad will fulfill his daughter's request—but only if it's the right gift, at the right time. Sometimes he may give the gracious gift of saying no. But always—always—he cares about his child's request.

In his classic book on prayer, C. S. Lewis puts it this way: "Someone said, 'A suitor wants his suit to be heard as well as granted.' . . . We can bear to be refused but not to be ignored. . . . The apparent stone will be bread to us if we believe that a Father's hand put it into ours."[2]

The more Mason and I prayed, the clearer my image became of

the God we were praying to. Perhaps he wasn't a stern father after all, with a snake in one hand and a stone in the other. Maybe he was more like a good dad—with a twinkle in his eye and his child on his back.

PART 6

Gratitude

My prayer is a cold little thing, Lord,
because it burns with so faint a flame.
But you are rich in mercy
and will not mete out . . . your gifts
in proportion to the dullness of my zeal.
But as your kindness is above all human love,
so let your eagerness to hear be greater
than what I feel when I pray.

ANSELM OF CANTERBURY

The Connecticut Yankee

❀

When my brother and I were little, our family lived on a dead-end street, so there weren't a lot of neighbor kids to play with. On top of that, the two girls up the hill were regularly in a huff with us, for reasons I never quite figured out. That meant that Kyle and I turned out to be each other's best playmates.

We'd spend hours together every summer, making elaborate tents out of old sheets, playing endless rounds of Life, and recording consecutive volleys in badminton or Ping-Pong. He'd teach me what he learned at baseball camp (thanks to him, I can still do my own rough interpretation of the crow hop), and I'd teach him what I learned in gymnastics. (At least until the infamous "Backbend Day," at which point Mom intervened, claiming I needed to stop, lest I break him.)

At any rate, Kyle and I had been buddies for a long time. So when he and my sister-in-law, Amber, moved to the East Coast, a little part of my heart broke. Several months later, when Amber cooked up a plan with one of her new friends to set me up with this friend's brother, I was excited on several levels. For one thing, everything I'd heard about him made him sound like he fell into the Good Potential category. And while I had a job I loved and good friends at home, there was the added incentive of possibly living near my brother one day.

Before my next visit, Amber's friend passed along my contact information to The Connecticut Yankee, and we arranged a time to get together. We weren't very far into the date before I discovered that he was something of a professional dater. He'd been on all the circuits— various online dating sites, speed dating, singles mixers. He'd even flown to California and Michigan to go out with girls who sounded promising online. He had this dating form down to a science by now.

"How about you?" he asked. "Have you tried eHarmony or Match.com?"

"No," I said. "I don't think I'm brave enough for that."

He laughed. "Well, you're brave enough to go out with me!"

He had a point. But as intimidating as it was to be set up, it felt infinitely more so to let a computer do the matchmaking. For one thing, at least each of us had a character reference before diving into this. Maybe there wouldn't be a spark, but the chances of one of us being a psychopath were greatly reduced.

Besides, what if the guys I was matched with created the profiles they wanted me to see, not ones that reflected who they really were? And for that matter, what if I did? It's human nature to try to suck in your stomach and show your best side to impress someone else, but the one-dimensional world of e-dating makes it easy for that facade to remain in place much longer than in the real world. Which led to my next reason: Two of my least favorite pastimes were getting rejected by someone and rejecting someone else. Why would I pay monthly fees to experience exponentially more of both?

I'd had enough blind dating experience to know that there are some people who may appear perfect for each other on paper (or on-screen) but just don't click in person. And I had to believe the flip side was true too: Surely there were people who didn't make sense according to carefully devised algorithms but would be right in person. Maybe I'd change my mind, but I didn't see myself creating an online dating profile anytime soon.

As I sat in the passenger seat and my date drove the winding Connecticut roads, I tried to subtly study him out of the corner of my eye. I decided my initial reaction landed squarely on middle ground. He wasn't unattractive, but he wasn't drop-dead gorgeous either, which on the heels of The Linebacker felt like something of a relief. And while he wasn't a conversationalist per se, he was clear in his communication about some key things, like handing me a map and showing me where we were going. "Since you're not from around here and you don't know me, I want you to feel safe," he said. *Maybe it's not love at first sight*, I thought, *but at least I feel respected.*

The two of us were hiking on a mountain trail, about five minutes into the walk, when The Connecticut Yankee revealed his dating strategy to me. "There are only three things I need to know to determine if a girl is the right one," he announced with utter confidence. "One, she needs to be a Christian. Two, she needs to love her family. And three, she needs to be active."

"That's it?" I asked. Part of me was feeling relieved at such lax requirements. (What? No theological grilling about Communion?) But another part of me felt miffed on behalf of the millions of women who fit that description—each of whom was unique and valuable and couldn't be quantified by such a simplistic checklist.

As we clipped along on our hike, the conversation came to a rather abrupt halt after we'd sufficiently covered the three aforementioned topics. I wasn't sure if that meant I'd passed all the requirements and he was satisfied, or if I'd failed and he figured it wasn't worth pursuing more info. But I didn't have much time to think about it—I was huffing and puffing up the steep Connecticut inclines, all the while wondering if I might be failing his third qualification at that very moment.

In an attempt to squeeze out some more conversation (preferably about something that didn't fit into any of the loaded categories), I asked, "So, what kind of music do you listen to?"

He listed off a few favorites and then said, "Can you believe we used to have to take physical music with us on trips? It's so nice to be able to load whatever songs I want on my iPod."

"I know," I said. "Someday our kids will laugh at how cumbersome we were with our giant CDs."

He stared at me, eyebrows furrowed.

I rewound my words, trying to figure out what I'd just said.

Oh, shoot. *Our* kids.

"Our kids . . . as in, the next generation, not our particular kids, like yours and mine . . ." The harder I tried to dig myself out, the deeper the pit became. This was not a case of inserting my foot in my mouth; it was more like my entire leg.

Finally there was only one thing left to do: I laughed. The Connecticut Yankee didn't.

It looked like it was time to head down the mountain.

On our hike back, I surreptitiously pocketed an Ebenezer rock to add to my collection when I got home. I didn't know if this was going anywhere, but I figured it couldn't hurt. At the very least, I was pretty sure I was going to need a reminder that God was here with me in the uncertainty.

By the end of our blind date, I still found myself on middle ground. If I'd had a three-point requirement checklist, he wouldn't have failed in any area. But at the same time, nothing inside me was itching to see him again.

We got together once more during my visit, and I was hoping round two would be clarifying. But alas, everything still seemed rather gray. We said our good-byes, with no mention of the future. I wasn't sure if I was relieved or felt just a twinge of disappointment, but mostly, things just seemed weirdly unfinished.

When I got home and checked my e-mail, I held my breath,

waiting to see if there would be a follow-up message from him. There wasn't, which was partly a relief—it meant I wouldn't have to figure out if I liked him enough to attempt a long-distance relationship. But there was also a part of me that wished I'd made enough of an impression on him that he'd want to get to know me more.

I couldn't help but think it would have been easier to have a clear no or a complete flop of a date. The problem with being stranded in the gray territory was that it left me second-guessing myself: What if I'd been more charming? What if I'd emphasized how well I fit his criteria? What if I'd have liked him more if we'd spent more time together? Should I have made it a point to e-mail him? What if I was missing something?

As the days turned into weeks, one thing became clear: I wouldn't be moving east anytime soon. Not for The Connecticut Yankee, anyway.

Confessions of an Ungrateful Heart

❀

I'M INDEBTED to my parents for countless lessons they taught me over the years: Finish what you start. Life isn't fair. Put yourself in the other person's shoes. This is the recipe for snickerdoodle cookies. Here's how to fix a flat tire (but call us before you do). But there was one lesson that stood out even more than the others as a consistent mantra throughout my childhood: Write your thank-you notes.

As a kid, I'd dreaded the post-Christmas tradition of writing thank-you notes to relatives who had given me gifts. I'd come up with any excuse I could think of to procrastinate. ("Seriously, you can't expect me to write a thank-you note on this stationery without a coordinating pink pen.")

I hated to admit it, but spiritually speaking, I hadn't changed all that much from the sulky girl who took her gifts for granted and acted lazy or, frankly, sullen about acknowledging the Giver.

I knew Scripture was pretty clear that gratitude isn't optional—it isn't something to do only when we feel like it: "Be thankful in all circumstances," Paul instructed (1 Thessalonians 5:18). But what does it look like to say thanks when you get something you didn't ask for, or when year after year, the one gift you want never appears under the tree?

One dreary Midwest afternoon I talked to my friend Leah, who lived in a quiet valley in the heart of the Colorado Rockies (with, I might add, her high school sweetheart and their two kids). From her back patio, the view was a ridge of snowcapped mountain peaks set against a sparkling blue sky. It was nothing short of breathtaking, as I'd seen in countless Facebook photos. As I looked at the flat, monotonous landscape out my own window, I couldn't suppress my pangs of jealousy.

When I bemoaned my mountain-less view to Leah, her response surprised me.

"You know, it's funny," she said. "But after living here for almost a decade, I almost don't see it anymore. It's just as beautiful now as when I moved here, but somehow it has become ordinary, everyday. I don't even notice unless I make a point of really opening my eyes."

When I hung up the phone, I wondered if the same thing was happening to me when it came to God's generosity. He was so faithful with certain blessings that they had become part of the scenery. True, he hadn't given me the husband I'd been asking for, but like a good dad, he'd given me so many other gifts I didn't deserve. Like friends who told me the truth and made me laugh. A family who knew my quirks and accepted me anyway. A Tuesday prayer buddy who let me blubber on a regular basis. A house that was starting to feel like home, red couch and all.

And while it was true that my office looked out over a flat horizon, it was also the place where I had the privilege of working at my dream job. I'd been an editor at a book-publishing company for a few years now. As a lifelong self-avowed bookworm, I could hardly believe I got paid to work with words all day and be surrounded by books and book talk and book people. I loved being able to work with authors and help them tell their stories—to be invited into that sacred space as a book was being born. I'd never set out to be a career woman, but here I was: a woman with a career, and as it turned out, this too was a gift.

Yes, sometimes my greatest blessings were so woven into the fabric of my everyday life that I no longer noticed them, or I failed to appreciate them because I was too busy looking for a blessing of another variety.

⁓

During Christmas break when my brother was twenty, he and four friends were driving home from a conference together. Kyle's friend was driving, and she didn't see the oncoming car as she was turning left. By the time the other car saw them, it was too late.

The car my brother was in was mangled beyond recognition, and all but one of the passengers were knocked unconscious, Kyle included. According to reports that came following the accident, most people drove by the scene, assuming there was nothing they could do or that an ambulance was already on its way.

But finally someone stopped and realized there were people still stuck in the mashed-up car. He was able to pry open one of the doors enough to extract my brother and his friends and help them across the street, one by one.

Just minutes later, after Kyle was standing safely on the other side of the street, the car they'd been in caught on fire.

That Christmas break my brother had the thank-you note of all thank-you notes to write. I remember him sitting at the computer, lungs patched up and stitches still visible just above his right eye, staring at the blank screen. How do you come up with words to say thank you to someone who literally saved your life?

Our stunted vocabulary is inadequate; our courage fails us for such a task. And how much more so with God, who risked everything—and gave us everything?

I always thought of my brother when I read the story about the men with leprosy who had ultimate gratitude to offer. According to the biblical account, this group of ten guys suffered from an awful skin disease—physical agony made even worse by the accompanying social quarantine. No doubt they'd spent long days and nights away from family and friends and had been ostracized from their religious community, dreaming of what it would be like to be healed, for this disease to disappear for good.

Then one day they saw Jesus. Maybe they'd heard rumors about him before; maybe they thought they had nothing to lose. But for whatever reason, they cried out to him: "Jesus, Master, have mercy on us!" (Luke 17:13). And he did. In that instant, with a simple look, he healed them. The story would be powerful enough if that were the end.

But Luke offers this epilogue, which gives pause to an ungrateful heart like mine: Only one out of the ten remembered to turn back and say thank you. "One of them, when he saw that he was healed, came back to Jesus, shouting, 'Praise God!' He fell to the ground at Jesus' feet, thanking him for what he had done" (Luke 17:15-16).

This man's life had been irrefutably touched by Jesus, and he responded with a grateful heart. I wanted to be the one out of ten. I wanted to be the one running back. The one falling at Christ's feet.

I found it interesting that when these men met Jesus, they didn't specifically ask for healing; they asked for mercy. And I had to wonder: If Jesus had asked them what they wanted, what would they have said? Would they have asked for healing, or would that have felt too impossible? Maybe they would have aimed lower.

Whenever I had encountered this story in the past, I'd assumed the other nine didn't say thank you because they were ungrateful snots, or if I was in a more charitable mood, because they were egregiously oblivious. But maybe the bigger issue was that they got something different from what they were asking. Maybe they weren't prepared for the miracle they received. They received healing and a glimpse of the Messiah, but they couldn't embrace it with gratitude because they weren't ready for it. C. S. Lewis says, "It seems to me that we often, almost sulkily, reject the good that God offers us because, at that moment, we expected some other good."[1]

How often did I respond the same way? I'd been asking God for a husband, but what if he was giving me healing instead? Or a glimpse of his character? Or more of himself?

Could I say thank you even if he didn't give me the miracle I thought I wanted, the miracle I was asking for?

"In affliction, then, we do not know what is right to pray for," Augustine said. "Because affliction is difficult, troublesome, and against the grain for us, weak as we are, we do what every human would do. We pray that it may be taken from us. However, if he does not take it away, we must not imagine that he has forgotten us. In this way, power shines forth more perfectly in weakness."[2]

As foolish as I felt, I got out my stationery (and yes, a coordinating pen). It was high time I wrote a thank-you note.

Dear Lord, thank you . . .

Why God Loves
a Good Story

MY BROTHER AND HIS WIFE were home for a visit, and we were gathered around Grandma and Grandpa's huge dining room table packed with aunts and uncles and cousins.

Kyle and I shot a glance at each other across the big dining room table. Dinner was long over, but Dad's siblings were gearing up for yet another nostalgic storytelling marathon. When we were kids, this was the point when we'd get antsy and ask to be excused so we could play games or explore the basement with its endless hiding places. We knew that once the stories started flowing, one tale would lead seamlessly into the next, and we'd be trapped at the table all evening.

My dad is one of twelve children, all born within an eighteen-year span. As kids they pretty much had free rein of the great outdoors, so there's no shortage of wild tales. There's the infamous account of the time they caught a rattlesnake and brought it home in the binocular case, the time they lowered Danny through the second-story window during bridge club—in his underwear, no less—and the time they launched themselves off the swing into a trash can filled with water. And then there were the countless trips to the ER—the time the tricycle ramp experiment went awry and Ruthie broke her arm, the time Paul ended up with stitches in his head after swimming in the city fountain. And of course there was the time they tried to cross the swollen Yakima River . . . in an old playpen.

We grandkids had heard the same stories over and over from the time we were old enough to sit at the table, and even the most dramatic of the tales had become commonplace. Nothing changed in the retelling, except perhaps for a few embellished details here and there, or my poor grandmother's fresh horror at the things her children had kept from her until they figured the statute of limitations had expired.

But now that Kyle's wife, Amber, had been added to the mix, there was suddenly a shift in the dynamic. I was starting to appreciate our "family canon" of stories in a new way through her fresh ears. As I watched her jaw hang open in wonder at the antics of our fearless (if slightly masochistic) relatives, the post-dinner storytelling session became the highlight of our get-together. My brother and sister and I found ourselves itching to tell the stories too—begging our aunts and uncles to fill in the newbie about one event or another and interjecting any details they might have left out.

At home by myself one evening not long after our family dinner, I felt that odd cocktail in my gut—one part gratitude for my wacky family and one part sadness that I didn't have anyone to share them with. I had no one to go home with at the end of the night to debrief what we'd just heard—and no children of my own to pass these stories on to.

In the midst of my funk, I came across this passage in Psalm 78— its own family canon, in a way:

I will teach you hidden lessons from our past—
    stories we have heard and known,
    stories our ancestors handed down to us.
We will not hide these truths from our children;
    we will tell the next generation
about the glorious deeds of the LORD,
    about his power and his mighty wonders. (verses 2-4)

It struck me how important it was to the Israelites to pass on their stories to the next generation. They wanted to leave their children and their children's children with a spiritual legacy—the stories of God's faithfulness and miraculous interventions in their lives. I imagined there were times when the kids must have rolled their eyes long after their lentil stew was gone, thinking, *Oh great, here we go again . . .*

Those stories, nevertheless, became woven into the fabric of their very souls. And I had to believe that as the younger generation grew older and as more place settings were added around the table, those stories started to take on an even richer meaning than before.

I wondered about my own spiritual canon of stories. I'd always shelved passages like this in the past, assuming with a pang that they didn't apply to me since I had no children of my own. But as I read the words again, I wondered if there was something deeper God was talking about than just parental baton-passing. What if the charge to share stories with "our children" and "the next generation" applied to me, too? What if God expected the training of the next generation to be the responsibility of *his* whole family, not just those with biological families?

If the charge was for me, I had some serious catching up to do. Did I keep a mental record of the times God had come through for me and worked in powerful ways in my life? And was I sharing those stories with the next generation?

He commanded our ancestors
    to teach them to their children,
so the next generation might know them—
    even the children not yet born—
    and they in turn will teach their own children.
So each generation should set its hope anew on God,
    not forgetting his glorious miracles
    and obeying his commands. (verses 5-7)

I guessed that meant I'd better be ready to share my God stories with my friends' kids, the junior high girls I mentored, and anyone else God might bring into my life.

And how could I do that if I didn't remember the stories myself? So I bought a leather journal with a ribbon bookmark and started recording the stories of God's faithfulness to me.

Then I began my rather bumbling attempt to share the stories. I told four-year-old Zach, in terms I hoped he could understand, about being scared of the dark as a kid and how my mom would pray with me and remind me that God was right there with me. I told the junior high girls at my church about the time I made fun of a girl's hair during band in seventh grade (if I had looked in the mirror at my mightily hair-sprayed bangs, it should have thwarted all comments directed at anyone else). I told them how awful I'd felt afterward and how I asked for forgiveness and how God had given me a chance later to make friends with the girl.

At some point in the story, I have a hunch they were rolling their eyes and thinking, *Oh great, here we go again* . . . But I just imagined that big dining room table at Grandma and Grandpa's house. And I told the stories. Again.

Forty Days of Uncloistered Life

LENT WAS AROUND the corner again, and I was feeling rather gun-shy. After the whole Lenten prayer journal debacle and the pain of the baby Heather would never meet, I didn't want to put myself out there a second time. Why set myself up to be hurt?

As Ash Wednesday crept closer on the calendar, marking the beginning of Lent, I was reading a book someone had given me about the desert fathers, of all things. I didn't mind a range of genres, but at the end of a long day of work, I typically liked to lose myself in a fictional world full of witty banter and high-bodiced dresses, so a book about a bunch of socially maladjusted holy men who had been dead for a couple of thousand years was pretty far out of my usual realm. But my friend was so insistent that I had little choice but to oblige.

To my surprise, I was hooked from the first chapter.

Though the desert fathers and mothers weren't perfect, they were spot-on in some areas that mattered most. They were willing to give up everything—even basic comforts like food and home—to keep their focus on Christ. They sold all their earthly possessions and gave the proceeds to the poor in exchange for simple lives in the desert—lives marked by manual labor, silence, prayer, and fasting.

Yet for all I assumed they'd be rather grumpy, given their austere circumstances, their writings are marked by profound gratitude. Abba Copres is known for saying, "Blessed is he who bears affliction with thankfulness."[1]

Then I came across a startling revelation in my reading: For the desert fathers and mothers, even Lent was a time for giving thanks. These forty days of sorrow were tinged with gratitude over all Jesus had given up for the people he loved. I had a tendency to sort my spiritual reflections into neat categories, savoring thankfulness every November and reserving penitence for Lent, but these early believers recognized how closely intertwined gratitude is with every event on the church calendar.

Furthermore, they realized that Lent wasn't a penitential season just for the sake of being penitential. Believers in the early church traditionally were baptized on Easter Sunday, and the forty days leading up to that day were a time for the new converts to fast and pray and repent in preparation. But strikingly, it wasn't just candidates for baptism who observed this solemn period of sacrifice during Lent. The other believers fasted and prayed along with them, as a reminder of their own baptism and as a sign of unity among the church.

The more I read, the more I realized I'd been thinking about Lent the wrong way. I'd been wondering what I could get out of it, if it would "work" for me, how it would deepen my faith. It was, in other words, all about me. Now the desert fathers were whispering in my ear, reminding me to look beyond my own navel, encouraging me to reconsider engaging with Lent this year.

And so I tried to look at my life through the eyes of those early believers. What would they see as the hindrances to my spiritual life? What comforts were holding me back from a deeper, richer connection with God and from tighter unity with my spiritual brothers and sisters? If I were to go out and talk with them in their desert caves, what one thing would they counsel me to give up for forty days?

I hardly knew where to begin. Through the lens of an ascetic, my life probably would look like a veritable Mardi Gras. As I asked God for wisdom, I suppose I was anticipating some rather grandiose instruction. (*Get yourself a camel and pack your sunscreen, because baby, we're going to the desert!*) So I was more than a little surprised when the answer came to me: *Give up your snooze button.*

My snooze button? Honestly, the idea seemed ridiculous, if not a little insulting. Those early Christians gave up homes, careers, families, and society at large, and I was supposed to give up my extra half hour of sleep that came in the form of nine-minute intervals each morning? But to be honest, there was a deeper issue at stake beyond my initial protests: I wasn't entirely convinced I could do it.

I tried to bargain with God, telling him I'd deny myself anything else—I'd eat nothing but vegetables, I'd forego coffee, I'd fast every Friday, I'd give away a big chunk of my money. But my snooze button? Heaven help me, I wasn't even *conscious* at that point of the day. How could I be expected to do something so hard? I didn't even know why it seemed like God was nudging me in this direction yet, but the call seemed undeniable.

If the desert fathers were teaching me anything, it was that the one thing you think you can't give up is probably precisely the thing you need to loosen your grip on.

So one particularly icy February, when all I wanted to do at 5:35 a.m. was burrow further under my covers, my Lent experiment began. My first step was to move my alarm away from my bed so I couldn't slap it in my bleary, semiconscious state. The next step was to turn up the volume so I wouldn't sleep through it, even as I prayed that the neighbor who shared a wall with me wouldn't call the association.

The final step, however, was the trickiest of all. I'd been learning from the early Christians that it wasn't enough to give up something or simply deny myself. If that was the extent of my sacrifice, I would soon slip back into my old ways—or fall into new, more creative vices. If I wanted to successfully give up my snooze button, I'd need to replace it with something else.

And so as soon as my fire-siren alarm went off each morning, I'd stumble downstairs and use the time I'd normally be snoozing to pray. I quickly realized that I couldn't make myself too comfortable, or I'd be asleep in no time, so I decided to pull out some desert father–style conditions for praying. Each morning I prayed on my knees—on the wooden floor, no less—for added snooze-proofing. This was new territory for a Protestant girl like me, and I'm pretty sure I wouldn't have made it a day as a monk.

I remember one day in particular when my prayers were even more incoherent than usual and my mind was wandering helplessly. I kept looking longingly at the comfy red couch, which was directly in my line of vision from the hard floor. I was officially a spiritual wuss.

Jesus, I'm so sorry. I pictured him hanging from the cross, dying for the likes of me, who would one day kneel in my entryway, whining over a hard floor and the loss of twenty-seven minutes of sleep.

That's when the prayer bubbled up from my throat, unbidden: "Break me of my comforts."

I had no idea what I was asking.

Over my lunch break that day, I checked my e-mail and found an invitation to join a group from my church on a two-week trip to Thailand. The purpose of the trip was to work alongside an organization in Bangkok that assisted women trapped in the sex industry. The group would be going to the red-light district and offering hope to the women there—connecting girls on the streets with an established organization and teaching English and practical skills to women who had gotten out of the industry and were looking to rebuild their lives.

My mouse hovered over the delete button before I'd even finished reading the message. *Now that's something I could never do,* I thought. *That would be so far out of my comfort zone.*

At that moment my right hand turned to stone. What had I just prayed that morning? "Break me of my comforts." *Oh, Lord, I didn't mean this.*

It would be out of my comfort zone to go up to an English-speaking stranger in my own neighborhood and strike up a conversation. Surely God wouldn't expect me to go all the way around the world to talk with "women of the evening" in a country where I didn't even speak the language. And even if we managed to communicate somehow, what on earth would we be able to connect about?

But I couldn't shake the coincidence of the timing, and I figured I should at least look into it before saying no. I sent a tentative message to the organizer of the trip and was surprised to get a phone call back almost immediately.

"When did you get that message?" he asked. "It was sent three months ago, and the group has already been formed."

I checked the date stamp on the e-mail, and sure enough, the sent date was months ago, but for some fluky reason, it hadn't shown up in my in-box until that day.

When I heard that all the plans were already underway, I breathed a sigh of relief. *Well, I tried,* I thought. *Maybe God just wanted to see if I'd be willing to say yes.*

"You know what, though," the leader said, "we've been talking in our meetings and saying it would be nice to have another female on the trip. We want to make sure there's a woman in each of the small groups we'll send out once we're there."

I gulped.

"It's not too late," he went on. "We're purchasing the tickets tomorrow. Can you let me know first thing tomorrow morning if you're in?"

Tomorrow? Praying from the safe, if uncomfortable, floor of my home was one thing. Buying a plane ticket to Thailand on a day's notice was entirely another.

Red-Light Redemption

TWO MONTHS LATER I found myself jet-lagged but jacked up on adrenaline and granola bars. Between the twelve-hour time difference and the fact that our "workdays" started around 10 p.m., my body wasn't sure if it was time for breakfast, lunch, dinner, or bed. And for that matter, I couldn't tell if the grumblings in my stomach meant I was ravenous or just plain tired.

But any hunger pangs waned when I saw the mystery meat the street vendors were selling. The raw seafood sat out in the sweltering heat in uncovered carts, surrounded by flies, and I wasn't sure I was ready to add a trip to the hospital to my mounting list of international adventures.

We went out to the red-light district in groups of three, armed only with the address of the place we were staying, a few key Thai phrases, and about twenty dollars' worth of Thai currency in our pockets. My heart was hammering so hard I was sure everyone else could hear it. I had been under the impression that we'd be hitting the streets with at least one representative from the organization, but our host assured us it was easier to connect with the women if we didn't go en masse. That left just the three of us non-Thai speakers (all I could remember in my jet-lagged state was how to say hello and ask where the bathroom was).

The idea was that we'd offer to buy a woman out for the night, meaning once she turned over the pay to the bar she worked for, she'd be free to go for the rest of the evening. We'd invite her to do something with us—go bowling or get coffee—so we could get to know her and introduce her to the ministry in Bangkok. For the cost of a mere twenty dollars in US currency, she wouldn't have to degrade herself. For one evening, at least.

As my group walked down the strip full of flashing neon, my stomach threatened to betray me, and this time I knew it wasn't just the raw seafood on the sidewalk. I was horrified to see women—most of them young girls, really—standing outside the bars selling themselves. The image in my mind of sex workers as streetwise, hardened drug addicts was shattered when I saw the faces of these girls, who looked no older than the junior high students I mentored back home.

Legally the girls were supposed to be eighteen to work, but the organization told us that many girls came to Bangkok at age thirteen or fourteen, sent from rural parts of Thailand by their families, who were desperate for money. The girls would send all the money they earned back home to support their parents and siblings.

We met Ning within five minutes of our arrival. I'd been so worried about knowing which girls to approach, but the problem was solved when Ning came right up to us. She stared with open curiosity, trying to figure out what to make of us. We didn't fit the stereotype of the other Americans who were there: mostly fifty-plus white males who seemed surprisingly unembarrassed to be exploiting girls a third of their age.

"Why are you here?" she kept asking.

I was shocked to hear how fluent her English was.

"More customers if you speak English," she said with a shrug.

We explained about the organization we were with—how it offered another way of life for women in her situation. She could get an education and vocational training, plus classes that covered basic life skills—cooking, sewing, budgeting, parenting. The missionaries were there because of love, because of Jesus. And so were we.

"You have dignity and worth, just as you are," we told her. "No matter how stuck you feel, there's a way out. There's a better life."

Ning could only shake her head, trying to figure out what the catch was, what agenda we were hiding. "You pay 600 baht for me . . . and you get nothing?"

As we got to know Ning over the next week, I was surprised to find that she and I had more in common than I'd imagined. We were both the oldest of our siblings, and we both came from tight-knit families. We loved to read. Each of us had a dimple on our right cheek. We both had a weakness for coffee. And we were both mystified but intrigued by the concept of a loving God who answers prayer.

Ning told us that she'd been suffering from severe stomach ulcers for the past several months, and she didn't know what to do. Even if she could scrape together enough money to go to the doctor, the bar owner would never let her miss work to get an appointment. We gave her some Thai money to cover the expenses, along with an offer of prayer.

Prayer was not unheard of in this predominantly Buddhist country, but there was one aspect of our perspective on it that seemed to shock Ning. "You mean your prayers go to your God's ears?"

As I heard myself explaining this personal God who sees us and hears our prayers and grieves over our pain, it felt like something was coming unfrozen in my heart. I realized I actually believed what I was saying, and I was flooded with gratitude. I had no idea if anything was making sense across cultural lines and language barriers, but I had a hunch that at the very least, my little sermon had hit one person in the audience. Me.

On our last night in Bangkok, my heart was heavy. I'd known going into the trip that I couldn't expect to see someone do a 180 in the span of a week. Our goal was simply to extend Christ's love and to introduce women to the ministry for long-term connections. But even so, it broke my heart to have to say good-bye to Ning, not knowing if I'd ever see her again. Not knowing if she'd have the courage to make a leap out of the broken, familiar life she knew and into the unknown—into a life of dignity and freedom.

As we paid her bar fee again for the last time, a word came to me, unbidden.

Redemption. I'd heard the term plenty of times, but until that moment it was just a church word. But under the garish neon lights of the strip, it suddenly meant something real, tangible, personal.

I realized in that moment that Ning and I had something fundamental in common.

Ning, you and I have both been bought out, I thought. *Someone else has paid the price to set us free. There's a new life available to us, if only we will seize it.*

That night as we were saying our good-byes, Ning gave me a huge hug and grabbed my hand. "There's one more thing I want you to pray for," she told me.

"Of course," I agreed.

"Pray for an American husband for me."

Oh. I hadn't seen that one coming.

After seeing the clientele of American men who were making their way through the red-light district, I was fairly certain that was *not* what she really wanted. But if God was all I avowed him to be, then I had to believe he was big enough to sort through our prayers and see the deeper longings underneath them. I had to believe he could somehow translate our requests and graciously give us what we truly need, not just what we think we want.

"I'll tell you what," I said. "I'll pray for you, and you can pray the same for me."

Ning gave a wide, dimpled grin.

"Okay." She flashed me the peace sign, then threw her arms around me in one final hug.

On the plane ride home, I had to smile at God's sense of humor. *So you had to send me eight thousand miles around the world to teach me about praying for an American husband, huh?*

Contentment, Like It or Not

"Is contentment the same thing as settling?"

I was back in Ruth's comfy chair, this time munching on coffee cake and blackberries.

"If you accept that God is in control of something, does that mean you have to *like* your circumstances?" I asked. "Let's say someone has cancer. Can they be content but still wish for a different version of reality?"

Ruth looked at me kindly, no doubt realizing this wasn't hypothetical, or about cancer, for that matter. But she was too nice to call me out on it.

Instead, she told me a story.

"When we were living in Brazil, our third child was born. He wasn't strong from the very beginning, and his little lungs struggled to get the air they needed. Then, when he was around a year old, he got sick. He kept getting weaker and losing weight. We'd written to our church back home, begging them to pray for healing.

"One evening after dinner, when I was rocking him, I opened a letter from a woman back home who had gotten some misinformation along the way. She said how sorry she was to hear that our son had died. My first thought was that this must be God's way of preparing me for what lay ahead."

A cloud came over Ruth's face for a moment. "Then I looked into my baby's face. He wasn't breathing, and this is the truth: His skin was blue."

Without the luxury of an ambulance, a hospital, or even a doctor in close proximity, she had Bob put on a pot of boiling water in hopes that the steam would help clear the baby's lungs. And then she did the only thing she knew to do: She held her son in her arms and prayed.

"In that moment, I had two equally powerful feelings," she told me. "I desperately wanted my son to live. But I also desperately trusted the Lord. I believed he knew what was right more than I did."

After a pause, she added, "I didn't think I was strong enough to lose my own child, but I figured that if God asked me to do that, he'd make me strong enough."

As I swiped at my cheeks, I felt my perspective gradually recalibrating. Here I was mourning the loss not of my own child who might die on the mission field but of an unfulfilled dream. And yet I wondered if I, too, could respond to the losses in my life with Ruth-style trust. Could I believe that God knew better than I did what was good and right? And could I believe that if he called me to walk a certain path, he'd walk it with me?

"So what happened?" I asked.

"He made it. That night he turned a corner and started getting stronger and healthier." Ruth smiled, her eyes glistening. "It was my Abraham moment."

If I had to nail down the top ten hardest-to-understand stories in the Bible, the account of God calling Abraham to sacrifice his long-awaited son, Isaac, would have to lead the list. Why would a good God ask one of his faithful followers to do something that seemed so contrary to God's nature . . . so downright cruel? Yes, ultimately there was a graceful finish to the story, but Abraham didn't know that when he started his hike up the mountain accompanied by his son and a large knife.

According to Timothy Keller, in the cultural and religious backdrop of Abraham's day, it was a given that every firstborn son belonged to God. Although these sons were to be bought back through sacrifice (Exodus 22:29; 34:20), they were still viewed as belonging to God—something of a down payment for the family's sins in the time before the Cross. So in reality, Keller contends, God wasn't asking Abraham to commit murder; he was asking him to lay down what rightfully belonged to God.

Still, Abraham was left in a quandary. He believed God was holy, so he must hand over his son. Yet he also believed God was gracious and would keep his promises. How could both be true?

As I thought about Abraham and Isaac making their way up the mountain, and as I thought about Ruth rocking her little son in their jungle hut, I marveled at the faithful obedience of these two heroes. How was Abraham able to put one foot in front of the other, knowing what he must do at the top? How was Ruth able to surrender her son into God's hands, trusting him regardless of what happened?

Abraham's story, at its core, is a beautiful foreshadowing of grace: "[Abraham] told his servants that '*we* will come back to you' (Genesis 22:5). It is unlikely he had any specific idea of what God would do."[1] But he clung to the hope that God would somehow stay true to his character.

And so it was for Ruth. She, too, knew what God was like. And she trusted him to stay true to his nature, even when she had no idea what he'd do. Maybe that's the definition of true contentment: choosing to rest in who God is, regardless of the circumstances.

I hated to ask the next question, but I had to know. "Um, Ruth, what if your son had died? I mean, would you still have been able to thank God if he didn't answer your prayer?"

Ruth stood up and gathered a stack of papers from the kitchen counter. "Take a look," she said.

I looked up at her, utterly baffled. What was she talking about? I scanned the letterhead, noting it was from her husband's doctor.

"Bob has been having problems with his memory for some time now," she told me. "I started noticing it when we were in the car. He's always been so good at directions, but he kept forgetting where he was going—even in familiar places. Then there were other problems—he'd ask the same question twice in a row and not be able to come up with words for common things."

She glanced at the stack of papers in my hand. "I'd been praying for a miracle, but we just got the results from the doctor."

I sucked in my breath. "Oh, no. It's not . . ."

"Yes," she said. "Alzheimer's."

I stood up to give her a hug, but it was mostly for my benefit. Ruth was grieving, but underneath it was a very real peace. She was content and . . . yes, grateful.

I had a long way to go, but I hoped I'd be like her when I grew up. And I hoped I wouldn't have to come within inches of losing my baby in the jungle to get there.

PART 7

Joy

O guiding night!
O night more lovely than the dawn!
O night that has united
The Lover with His beloved,
Transforming the beloved in her Lover.

SAINT JOHN OF THE CROSS

Mr. Paper-Perfect

❀

It had been almost a decade since I was a bridesmaid in my friend Brooke's wedding. She'd met her husband at the college we attended, and they'd gotten married shortly after graduation. After a wedding filled with navy-blue dresses and bouquets of pink, yellow, and purple, Brooke's parents came up to the head table and greeted all the bridesmaids. Her mom hugged me as if I were her own daughter. "It will be your turn soon," she assured me.

Brooke and I stayed friends over the years, and her parents and I kept in touch a bit through Brooke and through the occasional Christmas letter. Still, I was surprised to get a message from Brooke's mom one day that said, "Would you be up for getting together with an eligible man I know?" Apparently he went to their church, and she thought we had a lot in common. Was it okay if she gave him my e-mail address?

Why not? I was becoming increasingly wary about setups, but on that particular day, I was feeling rather philosophical about it. *What do I have to lose?*

I'd also just turned twenty-nine, a number that felt much more aggressive than twenty-eight. At twenty-eight, I could still comfortably convince myself I was in my midtwenties. But twenty-nine . . . well, there was nothing "mid" about it; it was clearly just biding its time until thirty.

Truthfully, I didn't think it was the age that bothered me as much as the incongruity with where I thought I'd be at this point in my life. *What would it feel like to turn twenty-nine if I were married with a baby?* I wondered. I longed to have someone who would be by my side for each new decade that came along—someone to do life with and get wrinkly alongside. But at twenty-nine, with no prospects, I felt like I was behind somehow. If I was ever going to catch up with my friends and my hypothetical life plan and my biological clock, I needed to get moving.

I didn't tell all that to Brooke's mom. I just said, "Yes."

In his first e-mail, Mr. Paper-Perfect was a true gentleman. He sent me his stats so there wouldn't be any surprises: "I'm thirty-two years old, five foot nine, and 163 pounds. I've been living in this city for 11.5 years." (I responded in kind but opted to skip the weight entry.) He researched restaurants and offered to drive out my way. Once we were shown to our table, he pulled out my chair, and he made it clear early on that he would pay.

As we talked, I realized that Brooke's mom was right—we did have a lot in common. We had both grown up in small towns. Each of us was the oldest of three, and we were close to our families. We attended strikingly similar start-up churches and were involved in similar hospitality ministries there. We both had younger brothers who were married and nieces around the same age. We read a lot of the same books, and we both listened to audiobooks during our commutes. Both of us had even grown up with dogs named Molly.

On the way home from dinner, I was already mentally compiling the list of similarities.

A couple of days later, Brooke called. "So how was the date?"

"Well, I'm not contemplating wedding colors or anything," I said. "But I will say this: That was the best blind date I've been on."

Brooke passed on the message to her mom. What neither of us bargained for was that her mom, in a well-meaning attempt to nurture things along, relayed my quote to Mr. Paper-Perfect at church the next Sunday.

I was mortified. Would he think I'd put her up to it? Surely he'd think I was some kind of desperate amoeba of a girl. I braced myself to never hear from him again.

But to my surprise, he called with another dinner invitation. "How about an Italian place I know about?" he said.

I made double sure the phone was hung up before letting my squeal escape.

When I arrived at the agreed-upon restaurant, I wasn't sure about the greeting etiquette. *Do I give him a hug? If I make a move and he doesn't, I'll be like a trapeze artist grasping at thin air.* At the last minute I chickened out, reaching for his arm instead. Unfortunately (but happily), he did go in for the hug. For an agonizing few moments we were all sharp angles. I am quite certain I have never had so many elbows in my life.

Gratefully, he brought in some levity. "Well, it looks like you passed the background check for the second date," he joked.

I laughed, but as we talked more I discovered that with the high level of security for his job, his roommate actually did have to get a background check.

"Believe it or not," he said, "anyone I live with has to get a background check." He looked at me a moment longer than necessary and then cleared his throat. "You know, uh, roommates."

Was there a hint of something there? I willed myself not to read into everything like the English major I am, scanning for foreshadowing and symbolism at every turn. "So . . . how did you meet your roommate?"

"Well, funny story," he said with a sheepish grin. "I joined the singles group at my church hoping to find a wife. God gave me a best friend instead."

Dinner at the Italian place was followed up with another date—this one at a seafood place. After date number three, we stood shivering in the cold in the parking lot, not ready to leave yet. He gave me a hug, and this time all our elbows were in the right spots. "I'll have to figure out what we're going to do next."

What! Not *if*! I repeated the words to myself all the way home.

But a week passed, and then another. We exchanged e-mails, but his were brief. Work was busy, he said. Church was busy. Life was busy. Finally I got a rather cryptic message from him. "There's something I want to tell you," it read. "But I'd rather do it in person."

Okay . . . My mind started swirling. What did he mean? This was either going to be really good or really bad. But as he made plans to take me to dinner at a nice steak house, I pushed aside my premonitions of gloom. Surely he wouldn't drop fifty bucks to tell me he didn't want to see me again. Right?

Right?

It's a pity I'd already placed my order when he broke the news, or I'd have considered ordering the lobster. And maybe the most expensive wine I could fake my way through pronouncing.

After we returned our menus to the waiter, Mr. Paper-Perfect hemmed and hawed and then awkwardly delivered his line. "I've been thinking," he said. "We just don't have much in common."

I sat there, utterly paralyzed but for my rapidly blinking eyelids. Was there a punch line to come? But no, it was clear from his vigilant avoidance of eye contact that this wasn't a joke. "I wanted to be sure to tell you in person," he added.

As my brain struggled to catch up with the words coming out of his mouth, I remembered a comment from an actress I'd read about recently. When talking about the romantic comedy she starred in, Sanaa Lathan said, "I think that's a lesson, that your heart is going to fall in love with who it's going to fall in love with, and it's not necessarily what's on paper."

I'm afraid I wasn't much of a conversationalist after that point, but it was no matter, because my date took it on himself to offer me insider's tips on the best online dating sites.

"There's this great service I've been using that sets you up for lunch," he told me. "There's no pressure at all—you just meet the person for an hour and then see where it goes. You should try it!"

A pit lodged itself in my stomach. *How is it possible for one party to think this is a flop and the other to have missed the memo?* I felt like I'd just eaten a main dish of disappointment with a side order of embarrassment. *If we'd had a chance to get to know each other better, would this have had the potential to become something?* I wondered. *After all, I can be the slow-to-warm-up/grow-on-you type.* But the humiliation factor kept my lips sealed. Maybe this was his way of saying he was out of my league. In any case, this wasn't digesting well.

I took the rest of my meal to go.

A Divine Canvas

I saw the T-shirt before I even walked past the threshold of the front door that sun-drenched Sunday in May. My parents, my sister, and I were visiting Kyle and Amber's house for the weekend, and I'm pretty sure my first squeal escaped from my lungs before I got out so much as a hello.

"Mom-to-be," Amber's shirt said.

"Happy Mother's Day," I told her when I was finally able to formulate a coherent sentence. Slowly the gravity of those words settled into my heart as I considered this tiny miracle, now apparently the size of a kumquat. (Not that this served as much of a reference point for me, but as I was learning, babies are apparently measured not in centimeters or inches but by various-sized fruits.)

"I thought you'd at least get inside before you noticed," Amber said, shaking her head.

I looked at my brother, quietly beaming in the midst of all the commotion. *He's going to make a really good dad*, I thought. *My brother's going to be a dad—my little brother*. And right there in the crowded foyer of their home, heartache collided with joy in an incomprehensible jumble.

In the rational part of my brain, I understood that my lack of this particular joy shouldn't take away from theirs, and that the two sets of circumstances weren't really connected. But I couldn't quite shut out the voice asking why, as the oldest, I wasn't the first one to enter the parents' club.

But the joy was there too. Grandparents-to-be, aunts-to-be, and parents-to-be, all tripping over each other, exclaiming congratulatory remarks and making predictions and rejoicing so loudly I wouldn't have been surprised if the neighbors came over wanting in on the winning lottery ticket.

Kyle and Amber had been wanting a baby for a while now. We'd walked with them as they waited and hoped, uncertain about the plans God might have for their future. And through everything, we'd been praying for a miracle—that God would bring a baby into their home, through whatever means he saw fit. Any baby embodies an imprint of the divine, of course, but we were asking for a real water-into-wine, parting-of-the-sea miracle.

So when we found out about this baby God was knitting together even at that moment, I was bowled over with joy. My brother was going to be a dad. My parents were going to have a grandchild. I was going to be an aunt. And there was no doubt about it: The hand of God was all over this. We would have our own miracle baby in the family. I loved her already.

(Yes, I was sure it would be a girl.)

It wasn't until I got in the car to make the long trip home with my parents and my little sister that the other side of the news fully hit me. As overjoyed as I was about this new addition for my brother and sister-in-law, it caught like a snagged hangnail whenever I thought about my own life. Their lives were marching forward: marriage, a home, a nursery, a family of three. Meanwhile, I was in the backseat of my parents' car, a throwback to childhood.

And I couldn't help but wonder how things would change now. Would Kyle and Amber move on, get busy with their own lives, find friends who were in their stage of life? And more to the point: Would I be left behind?

I'd always dreamed about having my own kids around the same time as my brother and sister, picturing the cousins as the best of friends who played together endlessly at Grandma and Grandpa's house. But at the rate things were going for me, that didn't look likely.

As I stared out the window, Dad's voice broke into my reverie. "Hey, guys, look behind us."

I turned around to take in one of the most unusual sunsets I'd ever seen. And perhaps *sunset* isn't even the right word. It was more like all the clouds in the Northern Hemisphere had decided to convene in one corner of the sky. Clouds of every shape and size were lined up in cascading layers of blue—from the faintest periwinkle to the deepest navy.

"You may never see a sky quite like that again," Dad said matter-of-factly.

"Forever—is composed of Nows," Emily Dickinson said.[1] Or maybe it's composed of skies. The sunsets and the storms. And everything in between.

A Family of One

I BLAME IT on the US Census Bureau.

I'd been embracing my anticipated aunthood and was learning to look for the joys in the present. Frankly, I'm pretty sure I would have been the picture of emotional health . . . if only that blasted survey hadn't required me to answer the nosy first question: *How many people live at your house?*

No matter how I diced it—wondering if I could include the occasional dinner guest or my mostly alive houseplants in my response—in good conscience, I could only check the box for that lonely, sharp-angled *1*. If it had been an essay answer instead of multiple choice, I would have said something about how my house felt so empty I sometimes talked out loud to myself just for the sake of conversation, how I felt swallowed up by my queen-size bed, how I ate dinner surrounded by three empty chairs as I worked my way through leftovers from the same dish all week.

In all fairness to said government office, which I'm sure is made up of plenty of lovely people, it was probably the sequence of events more than the questionnaire itself that provoked the meltdown.

It had all started over the weekend, when a friend from college was in town for a visit. I was attempting to hang pictures in my newly painted "goldenrod" bedroom, and my friend was helping me out. Or trying to, anyway. Between my ineptitude for all tool-related activities and my perfectionistic leanings, this project was driving me up the proverbial wall. It was just then that my friend, married for almost a decade, made the comment: "Well, I think it's good enough. It's not like you're having wild sex in here or anything."

Zing. I don't remember what I said once my voice returned to me, or if I had the composure to string any words together at all. I knew my friend loved me and would never intentionally hurt me. And at some point, when I got a little more distance, I was sure I'd be able to find the humor in it. But I wasn't there yet.

When my friend and I met at age eighteen, our lives looked pretty similar. We lived in the same dorm, took some of the same courses, had crushes on some of the same senior guys, liked the same foods, and jogged at about the same pace. But immediately after college graduation, our lives took significantly different turns—she got married a month after we got our diplomas, and I moved back in with my parents for a year. About the same time she moved into a sprawling house in a family-friendly suburb, I bought a cute but tiny condo with no backyard. She had two babies in close succession, and I switched careers. She celebrated her fifth wedding anniversary about the time I got set up on my fifth blind date.

It would have been easy to let the friendship slide, but we made it a point to get together about once a month to drink coffee and catch up on each other's lives. When she moved out of state, we set up phone dates to talk and pray together. The different life stages surfaced at times, but in some ways our friendship was the richer for it.

It's nice to have life-stage friends, we decided—people you connect with because it's convenient or you have obvious things in common. But there's something uniquely validating about being friends with someone who's in another place in life. We weren't friends because our kids played soccer together or because we found ourselves in the break room at work at the same time. We were friends because we saw the real person inside and loved each other for who we really were.

And so, on that fateful picture-hanging afternoon, I tried to remember the history we shared. Her comment stung, all right—not least of all because it was true. I *wasn't* having wild sex, or any sex at all. But it was a decision I'd made to wait until marriage, and I knew my friend supported my commitment. This was the bed I'd made for myself, so to speak, and now I was lying in it. Wobbly pictures overhead and all.

And I suppose when it comes down to it, that's the risk that comes with the territory of cross-life-stage friendships. No doubt there were times when I failed to empathize with her struggles in marriage and parenting too. But I had to believe the unexpected benefits of a friendship like this outweighed the minefields, because along the way, we were given glimpses of life in someone else's shoes—an opportunity to get to know someone who wasn't exactly like us, a chance to dispel illusions about how green their grass is.

Dietrich Bonhoeffer said that the defining characteristic of followers of Christ is that they bear one another's burdens. "It is only when he is a burden that another person is really a brother. . . . God took men upon Himself and they weighted Him to the ground, but God remained with them and they with God. In bearing with men God maintained fellowship with them."[1]

Before my friend left that afternoon, she asked me, as she often did, how she could pray for me. I told her that my baby sister and her boyfriend were starting to talk some specifics about the future, and I had a hunch there would be a ring soon. I admitted that although I was happy for her, I was having trouble acclimating to this unexpected order of things. I wanted to rejoice with her as she rejoiced, but I was struggling to dig deep enough to find that kind of gut-level joy.

When I opened my eyes after we prayed, I saw something unexpected and beautiful: My friend was crying.

"I'll keep praying for you," she said. "But it's okay if you need to say, 'This is crappy and not what I expected.'"

My decade-married friend who had never been the spinster older sister . . . she was willing to bear this burden with me.

And by some strange miracle, my load felt lighter than it had for some time.

That night when I went to bed, I still felt the echoes of a household of one. But my pictures were hung. And someone else was holding my loneliness with me, even from the other side of the marriage fence. Maybe the old saying was just about right: "The grass is greener where you water it." Even if you sometimes have to water it with saltwater tears.

Later that week I went to my friend Linnea's house to join her and her family for dinner. Little Ezra had just turned three, although considering the way he could run circles around me at Memory and recite the dietary habits of the brachiosaurus, you'd swear he was older.

That evening after dinner, Ezra was eating his "special treat" of M&M's, his reward for polishing off his serving of veggies. Linnea, always a math teacher, had him trained to count his M&M's as he ate each candy. We adults continued our own conversation as he popped chocolates into his mouth one by one.

When he got to the number four, Ezra said, "That's how many people are in my family." There was a pause as he looked at me, a bit puzzled. "Aunt Stephanie, how many people are in your family?"

I opened my mouth to say, "One," but nothing came out. The poor kid looked at me, baffled, no doubt pitying the mathematically challenged grown-up who didn't yet know how to count.

Most of the time, I didn't mind living alone. I could eat whatever I wanted for dinner, whenever I wanted to. I could hoard the covers and press the snooze button in obnoxious repetitions, and there was no one to complain about it. No one left the toilet seat up at night for me to fall into, no one expected me to do their laundry, and I was never responsible for carpool duty.

Still, as I looked into that three-year-old's big blue eyes, I didn't know how to explain to him that there was just one person in my family. Besides, I wasn't sure I could get any words out past the pesky knot in my throat. Did a family of one even constitute a family?

As I was formulating my response, I was vaguely aware that Ezra was popping M&M number five into his mouth while narrating more of his own little commentary.

"But pretty soon we're going to be a family of five, because Mommy has a baby growing in her tummy."

Wait.

I was jolted out of my internal mathematics as I rewound Ezra's words.

"Did he just say what I think he said?" I looked at Linnea, and sure enough, she was beaming.

"It was supposed to be a secret," she said. "But to tell you the truth, I'm glad it slipped out."

I gave Linnea a hug and thought about how full her life was. She would soon have three kids under the age of four, which translated to a very full mom-plate. She'd have full bedrooms, a full car, full diapers, an even fuller schedule.

When I got home, I pulled out my Bible and a bag of chocolate. (I needed more than my household head-count quota of M&M's for an announcement like that.) I opened to John 10, trying to make sense of the verse about fullness in a place where emptiness seemed to echo off the walls: "I have come that they may have life, and have it to the full" (verse 10, NIV).

As I looked at the words, I was a little surprised by the context of Jesus' statement. He mentions it in the midst of a parable about sheep—how he's the Good Shepherd who calls us by name and brings us to rich pastures. He goes on to talk about his other sheep and how there will be "one flock with one shepherd" (verse 16).

It doesn't seem like a coincidence that when Jesus talks about the full life he intends for us, he describes it in the context of community, of his united flock. He doesn't compare us to a lone wolf wandering solo in the night. No, the full life is found inside the gate, with all the sheep in there together.

As a family of one, I could embrace parts of the abundant life that my friend couldn't. And there were aspects of abundance that Linnea, as a mother of 2.5 kids, could experience that I couldn't. But we were both sheep in the same pasture, led by the same Shepherd. He'd brought us into the same pen on purpose—so we could share those pieces of life with each other. I could share my quiet home as a respite for her when she needed a break. She could share her children and their bursting energy with me. And in doing so, we both got a fuller, richer taste of life—and of the Good Shepherd himself.

But in ten years, when the Census Bureau sent out their cold, cruel survey again, I surely hoped I could check a number other than one. Or at the very least, that I'd have a family-size bag of M&M's on hand.

Full of Grace

A FEW MONTHS before Amber's due date, Mom and I hosted a shower for Amber and Baby Girl (I was right!). The shower was overflowing with pink azaleas and all of Mom's famous brunch foods—bacon-egg casserole, raspberry coffee cake, and her heavenly hash browns. Everyone said heartfelt prayers for this little miracle and shared the characteristics of Kyle and Amber that they hoped would be passed on to this new life.

I was having moderate success focusing on my role as shower hostess and aunt-to-be and was feeling pretty proud of myself that I hadn't so much as smudged my mascara. But when Amber opened the gift from my grandmother, it was game over. There was an almost reverent hush as my sister-in-law unwrapped the package. When the tissue paper was peeled away, she held up a family heirloom, a knickknack hand-painted by my great-grandma and given to my grandmother when her first baby was born. Now it would be passed on to a new generation.

I grabbed my camera, partly to capture the moment and partly to give my hands something to do.

I sucked in my breath. How could such sweetness and such sorrow be captured in a single frame? I knew how precious this was—this snapshot in time with four generations present. Yet I wasn't one of the moms in the legacy.

Rejoice with those who rejoice. The words came to mind without warning, without invitation.

Rejoice *with.* What did it mean, I wondered, to rejoice *with* others, not just to rejoice *for* them? That seemed like a much loftier call. With a little effort, I could probably be happy for people who had occasion to be happy. But to be happy *with* them?

I snapped another shot of Amber and her growing belly. I had a feeling this lesson was going to have a rather lengthy gestational period.

On a blustery December day, just a few weeks before the baby was due to make her appearance, I was lost in holiday blues. *Is Christmas so hard because it's a reminder that another year has passed and here I am, still in the same spot?*

Still single, some 360 days and several dashed hopes later, with nothing to show for it other than a few flopped blind dates.

As I put the key in the lock of my dark town house, I was startled to hear something clatter to the ground. *What on earth?* I picked up a package that was covered in several layers of plastic grocery bags. Underneath was plain brown wrapping, secured with masking tape. I searched the package for a tag or a note. Nothing. I was stymied. Who would leave something for me on the porch with no label? I peeled off the paper.

I saw the back side first. An old piece of art, by the looks of it. When I turned the frame around, my gaze landed immediately on the woman's eyes.

It was a simple oil painting of a young Mary with her infant Son—a common enough subject—but what struck me was how *human* Mary looked. There was no halo, no fine clothing, no glowing scene in the background. Just simple Mary, holding her Son and looking up toward heaven. And those eyes! Her look captured a curious blend of questioning and surrender—as if she didn't quite understand this task she'd been called to, but even without answers, she was ready to accept it.

I hung the picture up, still wondering who it was from. Every time I looked at Mary's face, I wondered what things she must have "pondered in her heart."[1] Did she ever tell God, when Joseph decided to divorce her, that all she'd wanted was a straightforward road to happiness—to be loved by a good man, to settle down near her family and friends, to have a family of her own? Did she ever resent being called to something so undoubtedly different from the life she must have imagined for herself?

A few days later I got a phone call from my aunt—the youngest of Grandma's dozen. "I meant to call you earlier," she apologized. "The picture was your grandma's—the one that hung on the wall in her room when she was a kid."

I imagined Grandma as a redheaded girl, the oldest of her siblings, the little mom. Her father, the owner of a saloon, struggled to provide for his family during the worst years of the Depression. As finances grew increasingly strained, alcohol clenched its grip tighter on him. When her mother became ill with polio when Grandma was a teenager, she was left to manage the household, put meals on the table, and get her younger siblings off to school each day. I pictured her in her room at night, kneeling by her bed to say her prayers: "Hail Mary, full of grace . . ."

I grew up in a faith tradition that went so far out of its way to avoid deifying Mary that we all but ignored her (with the lone exception of her annual appearance at the crèche—demure and in blue, always in blue). So I wasn't quite sure what to do with Mary. Looking to the Gospel of Luke for clues, I read the few paragraphs where she appears in the story of the Incarnation.

When I got to the angel's words to Mary, I stopped in my tracks: "Hail, full of grace, the Lord is with you!" (Luke 1:28, RSVCE). I guess I'd always figured Mary was chosen and deemed grace-full because she was somebody special, someone worthy of her call. But maybe Gabriel was calling out the specialness, the worthiness, of the one *inside* her. Maybe when Gabriel said "full of grace," he meant it quite literally, because at that very moment, she had Grace himself growing within her.

I was under no illusion that this life God was calling me to—this life so different from what I'd dreamed of and planned for—held anything near the gravity of Mary's assignment. But maybe I could take my cue from her response anyway. When life wasn't what she expected, this girl responded with a single question: "How can this be?" And then she surrendered with joy and obedience: "Behold, I am the handmaid of the Lord; let it be to me according to your word" (Luke 1:34, 38, RSVCE).

I had something gestating inside of me, too. When it came time for my soul to give birth, what would I discover I was full of?

When Joy Comes in Camo

With each passing Tuesday, Mason and I were praying by baby steps, gradually stepping further into the swirling waters of prayer. But even as we went deeper, nothing seemed to budge. Tuesday after Tuesday we showed up with our door-banging, persistent requests but got no answer.

A guy who had been showing interest in Mason completely flaked out—ceasing all communication without explanation. And on the heels of my Mr. Paper-Perfect, with no new prospects in sight, I was feeling rather low on the hope meter myself. We ticked off all the women we knew who were smart, attractive, mature, and generally pleasant to be around . . . yet mystifyingly single.

That's when we uttered the most futile prayer of all.

Why?

At some level I knew that such a question is a little like trying to calculate the breadth of the sky using a yardstick. But I couldn't stay away.

Why does the wait have to be so long?

Why don't you step in and do something?

Why are you withholding this good thing?

If you're a good Father who loves his children, why are you saying no?

One Tuesday Mason pointed out that maybe we weren't the only ones haunted by that question. In a surprising number of places, it turns out, the psalmists ask it straight to God's face.

O LORD, why do you stand so far away?
    Why do you hide when I am in trouble?
PSALM 10:1

You are God, my only safe haven.
    Why have you tossed me aside?
Why must I wander around in grief?
PSALM 43:2

Wake up, O Lord! Why do you sleep? . . .
Why do you look the other way?
    Why do you ignore our suffering and oppression?
PSALM 44:23-24

The more psalms I read, the more I was struck by their brutal honesty—how unabashed the authors were about expressing the whole range of human emotion. They didn't whitewash things—they put their feelings out there, raw and "unspiritual" as they might be. By my reckoning, some psalms seemed to be little more than sobs put to paper.

And it was a relief.

I was glad that God wasn't scared away by my whys and my ugly emotions and that he wasn't going to wag his finger at me for bringing them to him. But as I kept reading, I noticed an interesting pattern. The psalms never answered why. Instead, they answered another question: *Who?*

Who is this God we're praying to?

Who am I in relation to this big God?

Who is walking beside me on this journey, whether my song sounds more like lament or joy?

The LORD is king forever and ever! . . .
LORD, you know the hopes of the helpless.
    Surely you will hear their cries and comfort them.
PSALM 10:16-17

I will put my hope in God!
    I will praise him again—
        my Savior and my God!
PSALM 43:5

Rise up! Help us!
    Ransom us because of your unfailing love.
PSALM 44:26

This *who*, in other words, is the God who saves, the God who ransoms, the God who helps. He is a forever kind of God who hears the cries of his children and then does something about them. He is the God who loves without fail. With a *who* like that, you can trump a whole lot of *whys*.

I'd recently read about Julian of Norwich, the fourteenth-century Christian mystic who found herself in the midst of a spiritual dry spell some seven centuries ago. This is what she sensed God saying to her in that season: "Pray wholeheartedly though you may feel nothing, though you may see nothing, yes, though you think that you could not, for in dryness and in barrenness, in sickness and weakness, then is your prayer most pleasing to me, though you think it almost tasteless to you. And so is all your living prayer in my sight."[1]

One Tuesday Mason and I had walked to our favorite park bench to pray—the one that was least likely to invite interruptions from kids swinging on the playground, casual joggers, and overly friendly dogs. We prayed out of our lament, out of our dryness, out of our barrenness. Our circumstances had felt particularly lament-worthy that day, and we had some mascara damage to take care of before we headed back to work.

Then, as we were walking back, Mason's belt suddenly fell entirely off its presumably secure location around the middle of her sweater. She was about three steps past the unlikely hula hoop, which was now on the sidewalk, before we realized what had happened.

There was something about the scenario that struck us as so ludicrous—to go in an instant from a state of lament to a state of beltlessness—that we found our sides splitting mid-sidewalk, dogs and playing children momentarily forgotten. Maybe it was a simple case of catharsis. Or maybe God was answering our prayers with something we never would have expected.

Laughter.

As Garrison Keillor says, "God writes comedy but sometimes has a slow audience."

The belt incident, ridiculous as it was, felt like a tangible reminder that while God cares about the details of our lives, he also doesn't take us too seriously. Heaven knows I had that covered for all three of us. I wondered if part of the gift of holy laughter is the perspective it offers about how big God is compared to our limited human vantage point. Augustine posed just such a query to God: "Do my questions make you smile at me and bid me simply to acknowledge you and praise you for what I do know?"[2]

I pictured God cracking up on his celestial throne and, in the kindest way possible, telling his two daughters that, yes, sometimes we need to come to him in honest lament. And other times we need to stop taking ourselves so seriously and laugh about the comedy he's writing.

∾

My mom's parents were in town, having taken the train on a several-day journey from Washington State. My parents, grandparents, siblings, and I all squeezed into a cabin a few hours away for the long weekend, trying to soak up the time together before everyone scattered to all points on the compass—my grandparents out west, my brother and his family on the East Coast, and my sister up north.

On Sunday morning we decided to have our own informal church service. Over steaming mugs of coffee, we went around the room and each of us shared how we'd seen God at work in the previous year. When it was Grandpa's turn, there was an awkward pause as he sat there, the proverbial deer in the headlights. Mom and I exchanged a glance across the room. He wasn't going to be able to do it.

The dementia had crept in slyly at first, disguised as the typical forgetfulness that comes with aging or excused away by tiredness or stress. But at my brother's wedding, when Grandpa got behind the wheel and couldn't remember where he was or what he was supposed to do, we realized something more significant was happening. Denial was no longer an option.

Over the past few years, we'd watched Grandpa progress through the stages of dementia: gradually being robbed of his short-term memory, losing once-familiar words and names of objects and people, and on the bad days, being stripped of the ability to recognize even the people he loved most.

When I was a child, I was in awe of my grandfather's superpower-like ability to retain information and recite it back verbatim. He grew up in an era when education by rote was in vogue, and even after seven decades, he could still conjure up full-length poems by William Wordsworth, quote entire chapters of Scripture, and recite everything from schoolyard ditties to complex scientific theorems.

I looked at Grandpa and winced as I saw his face contort with frustration. A decade earlier, he would have been facilitating this whole conversation. Now he opened his mouth several times, but each time no words came out. Should I step in, I wondered, and save him from the embarrassment of being put on the spot to do something that was now beyond his capabilities? Or would that only make him feel more shame? His eyes started to brim with tears, and I turned my head. I couldn't bear to see him suffer like this.

Just as I was getting ready to jump in and deflect the spotlight to the next person, I heard a familiar yet unexpected sound—the deep baritone of Grandpa's voice. Somehow, for the moment at least, he knew every word of the familiar hymn he'd sung for the past eighty years, since those Sundays when he'd sat in that tiny church in rural Montana.

What a friend we have in Jesus,
All our sins and griefs to bear . . .
Jesus knows our every weakness,
Take it to the Lord in prayer.

And in that moment, as the words wrapped around me like a blanket, I had a glimpse of what it was to hold joy and lament in my hands at the same time. Maybe that's what it means to be joyful always, as Scripture so mystifyingly commands. Not that we have to ignore the griefs that are ours to bear, but that we actively seek out the golden threads of joy woven right in the midst of them.

Somewhere along the way I'd gotten the idea that joy was a conditional state—something that ebbed and flowed with the tide of circumstances.

Joy equals being loved by a good man and having someone to live life with.

Joy equals snuggling a chubby, pink-cheeked baby in my arms.
Joy equals dreams come true.

But Scripture says that true joy doesn't have to ebb and flow with our circumstances. It's something we have the power to choose, no matter what: "*Always* be joyful" (1 Thessalonians 5:16, emphasis added).

That deceptively simple verse forced me to ponder that perhaps joy isn't determined by the winds that blow into our lives after all. We just have to dig a little deeper in some situations. Saint John of Avila said, "One act of thanksgiving, when things go wrong with us, is worth a thousand thanks when things are agreeable to our inclinations."

Thank you, God, for these good moments, for these joys. Whether they're agreeable to my inclinations or not.

Bone-Crushing Happiness

❀

WHEN MOM CALLED with an update about Pastor Bob and Ruth, I assumed the trouble was with Bob and his advancing Alzheimer's. I was wrong.

"It's Ruth," she told me. "She broke her neck last night."

Ruth had been struggling with osteoporosis for years but had managed to maintain a relatively normal life despite the diagnosis. All that changed, however—literally overnight. Ruth had gotten up in the middle of the night, and when she returned to bed in the dark, she'd misjudged where she was. Her brittle bones were no match for the hard floor.

"The doctor says the prognosis isn't good," Ruth told me when I visited her after she was released from the hospital. She was in an enormous cast with metal all around her head and down her spine and an immobilizing ring of white plaster around her neck. As I looked at her, I had to think that a getup like that would make a straitjacket seem like a comfortable alternative.

"My bones are too weak for surgery," she told me. "They said I'll have to wear this cast the rest of my life. If I take off the cast or make one wrong move, I'll be completely paralyzed."

My eyes filled as I thought about all Ruth would miss out on. She could no longer embrace her husband, hug her children, pick up her grandchildren, or even turn her head. She couldn't bake cookies or drive a car or live a normal life. *Really, God?* She still had so much to share with the rest of the world. It didn't seem fair.

At that moment Ruth's steady voice intercepted my thoughts. "I told the doctor to wait and see. I believe God is going to do a miracle here. I'm *not* going to wear this thing the rest of my life."

Ruth winked at me. "Could you get that book off the coffee table and bring it over here?"

I obliged, though I had no idea what this oversized, yarn-bound book had to do with our conversation.

"You can turn the pages," she told me. "I'm supposed to limit my arm movement."

I opened the book to find a scrapbook of sorts chronicling her and Bob's life together. The pages were sprinkled with ticket stubs from voyages across the ocean, church bulletins from special occasions, and photographs with black-cornered edges that captured their life from the 1950s on.

There weren't many captions, but Ruth provided her own fascinating commentary, recounting her adventures as I turned each page. When she and Bob were first married, they planned to farm their land in South Dakota, as their parents and grandparents had before them. They were passionate about mission work, and they planned to send as much of their income as possible to support organizations overseas. But it wasn't long before they both felt God nudging them not just to give but to go. And so, with one baby in their arms and another on the way, they packed up all their belongings and said tearful good-byes to their families, knowing they might never see their parents again on this side of heaven.

They spent ten years in the jungles of Brazil, learning the culture and loving the people with Christ's love. But when the vision of the organization they were with shifted from empowering the nationals to forming Western-led churches, Ruth and Bob knew it was time to move on. They went back to the States with four children, no job, and no place to live.

It wasn't long before God made it clear that although the door had closed in Brazil, he wasn't finished with them. They moved into the heart of Chicago, where they pastored a church, raised a family, and launched a booming high school ministry. After their time in Chicago, they were called to pastor a church in the suburbs, where they brought life and energy to a church in desperate need of some spiritual CPR.

"It's interesting," Ruth said as we got to the end of the scrapbook. "Just when we started putting down roots, God would call us to a new place. And I'm a person who really likes roots."

She looked at me thoughtfully. "I was surprised to find that I could be happy in any of those places. In the old drafty farmhouse, when we didn't have money and I painted the kitchen walls red to make it cheerier. In our dirt-floored home in Brazil, where the bugs crawled through the walls. In the middle of the city, where it was hard to find any green patches of land. And in this beautiful townhome we have now."

"All Joy reminds," C. S. Lewis said. "It is never a possession, always a desire for something longer ago or further away or still 'about to be.'"[1]

Maybe joy isn't something that makes its debut once all your circumstances line up just right. Maybe it's something you can soak up no matter where you are. Even when you have an immobilizing cast on your neck.

And if that was true, then surely it was true if you had seven rocks in your little pouch reminding you that the current tally was blind dates: 7; boyfriends: 0.

PART 8

Journey

*Nothing could be safer or less likely to lead us
astray than the darkness of faith. Do we insist
on knowing which way to go in this darkness?
Go wherever you wish—it doesn't matter. No one
can get lost when there is no road to be found.*

JEAN-PIERRE DE CAUSSADE

Limo Dude

My friend Sharon had been faithfully petitioning God to bring me a husband for a long time. Having been left by her first husband with three little kids some twenty years ago and recently remarried to a kindhearted true gentleman, she knew firsthand what the waiting ache feels like. She had seen God restore the years the locusts had eaten, and she wanted the same for me.

So when she mentioned that a man she knew was interested in meeting me for coffee, I agreed. With seven flopped blind dates under my belt, I knew better than to hold my breath, so I tried to parcel out my oxygen, even as my matchmaker gushed about the possibilities. But Sharon's enthusiasm was contagious, and I found myself getting swept along for the ride.

Unfortunately, the evening got off to a bit of a rocky start before I even met Limo Dude. He drove a Lincoln Town Car for a limo service, and he wasn't sure what his hours would be ahead of time.

We tentatively agreed to meet at 7:00 on a Friday evening. By 6:45 I was dressed and ready to go, with the characteristic blind-date knot in my stomach. Just as I was getting ready to walk out the door, my phone rang. He was going to be late.

"How about 7:30?" he asked.

I was as fidgety as a schoolgirl before summer break, eventually giving up on my book once I realized I'd been reading the same sentence for a good ten minutes. At 7:15 my phone rang again.

"I'm sorry, but it looks like it'll be more like 8:00," he said.

Take a breath. "Okay."

This went on, in consistent half-hour increments, until finally, a little before 9:00, we met up at the agreed-upon coffee spot.

As soon as we met by the front door, Limo Dude said, "I need to return these CDs to the library. Do you mind if we drop them off first?"

I hesitated, pondering the generally accepted advice that you shouldn't accept rides from strangers. But then I looked at his music stash and saw that he was armed with Christian classics like the Newsboys and old-school Amy Grant. Maybe we wouldn't be swapping a lot of music, but I felt pretty confident that kidnappers don't have "Friends Are Friends Forever" as the sound track for their nefarious deeds.

When we got to the now off-duty Town Car, I went to open the front passenger door. But as soon as I'd grasped the handle, Limo Dude stopped me.

"No, no," he said. "Let me give you the full treatment." And he proceeded to open the back door.

So our first real conversation wasn't face-to-face, or even side by side. It was conducted through the rearview mirror.

To my relief, we arrived at the library as promised. But when we made our way into the lobby, Limo Dude handed me the enormous Rubbermaid tote filled with CDs. "Here," he said. "Would you turn these in while I make a phone call?"

Okay, I thought. *Not exactly what I'd expect for first-date etiquette, but I'll try to cut him some slack.*

After our stop at the library, it was, to my relief, time to head back to the coffee shop. But this time as we approached the Town Car, I decided to nip the awkward chauffeur routine.

"Really," I said, "I think I'd be more comfortable in the front, if that's okay."

But he wouldn't hear of it. Into the backseat I went again.

We eventually made it to our destination, and we chatted for about an hour. I confess that between the delay, the unexpected turn of events, and the fact that I was nearing my bedtime, I was off my A game. I asked a few lackluster questions, but clearly my heart wasn't in it.

As I drove home (in the driver's seat of my own car), I wondered if we'd see each other again. I wasn't particularly interested in a second date, but I wasn't sure how to determine what constitutes a deal breaker. Yes, he was late, but at least he let me know. And I'm sure his reasons were legitimate. And true, there were no fireworks, no chemistry. (He was, however, a safe driver, and I'd be happy to recommend him to you in that capacity, should you ever find yourself in need of a ride to the airport in the backseat of a Lincoln Town Car.) But I'd heard of plenty of couples who "grew to love each other." What if I'd misjudged him? What if he'd just had a bad night? Should I give him another chance?

And then there was the person I felt worst for: Sharon, who had set us up. If I decided there was no chance that this could work, I'd feel like I wasn't just letting Limo Dude down; I was letting her down too. Hopes were splintering all around me and inside me, and I felt responsible somehow.

Was there any point in hoping and praying about this whole husband thing after all? With all the real problems in the world, like ethnic genocide in Sudan and the trafficking of women in Thailand, didn't God have bigger things to worry about than my flopped limo ride and my manless state? Besides, if I didn't get my hopes up, I wouldn't have to be disappointed when God didn't answer. And neither would my praying friend Sharon.

"Hope," my friend Sarah once told me, "is a shiny diamond of a thing." I knew what she meant. Beautiful to gaze on, but pity the person who falls on its sharp edges. From a distance, hope sparkles and shines, tantalizing you, beckoning you ever closer. But it's no safe place to land, as the very edges that reflect the light are sharp enough to cut you straight through.

Sucking Out the Marrow

During the final semester of our senior year in college, Sarah and I pasted a quote by Henry David Thoreau to the refrigerator of our little apartment: "I wished to live deliberately . . . and not, when I came to die, discover that I had not lived. . . . I wanted to live deep and *suck out all the marrow* of life."[1]

We were responsible students—probably overly so—and we were all too aware that our college years were racing by. If we weren't intentional about it, all our memories of our time on campus would be of writing and rewriting literary analyses of Joseph Conrad and perfecting diagrams of sentences with adverbial phrases.

So we made it a point to regularly encourage each other to squeeze as much life as possible out of our last few months in school, knowing that all too soon we and the rest of our friends would be parting ways and scattering across the country. Should we make the 11 p.m. run to Taco Bell with our friends? *Yes! Suck the marrow out!* Should we go with a group of friends to the James Dean festival? *Absolutely! Suck the marrow out!* Should we wear wigs and 1970s dresses out in public, pretending such behavior was perfectly normal? *By all means! Suck the marrow out!* Meanwhile, we dreamed about the future: how we'd get married to guys who were fast friends; how we'd live in the same cul-de-sac and our children would play soccer together in the street; how we'd travel the world together, starting with Italy.

It had been a number of years since our marrow-sucking days, and Sarah and I had both found our way into the normal grooves of work and adulthood. Sarah and her husband were settled in Seattle, and I was several thousand miles away in Chicago. We still got together when we could, but for the most part the wigs and crazy clothes stayed securely in boxes stashed in the back of our closets.

Then one cold blustery day in January I finished reading *O Pioneers!* by Willa Cather. When I got to the final page, a dam inside me that I hadn't known was there burst open. Maybe it had something to do with the fact that the year ahead would mark the big 3-0 for me. As long as I was safely in my twenties, the dearth of marriage prospects didn't seem quite so dire. Still plenty of eligible men out there, still plenty of fertile eggs left. But somehow thirty was starting to rhyme with "old maid" in my ears.

This is perhaps not the frame of mind one should be in when reading Willa Cather.

In the book, the protagonist, Alexandra Bergson, inherits the family farm after her father's death. She devotes her life to making the farm succeed in the face of unforgiving droughts, brutal Nebraska winters, financial strain, demanding physical labor, and loneliness. She sacrifices her whole life at the altar of duty and responsibility, failing to embrace the love right in front of her and forgetting to suck the marrow out of life. When the man she truly loves leaves for Alaska, she closes off a part of her heart, stoically resolving to do life by herself: "She began to wonder whether she would not do better to finish her life alone. What was left of life seemed unimportant."[2]

It isn't until the end of her life that she allows herself the luxury of letting others in, being happy, embracing life. The words she buried deep within her a lifetime ago are finally coming true: "People have to snatch at happiness when they can, in this world. It is always easier to lose than to find."[3] As the book comes to a close, Alexandra and Carl are finally together, after decades apart. Carl reminds her that their lives are part of the old story that keeps being rewritten. "It is we who write it," he says, "with the best we have."[4]

I called Sarah immediately, my voice shaky. "We have to go to Italy," I said. "Not someday—*now*. If we don't go now, I'm afraid we'll never go, and we'll be seventy years old in wheelchairs and then it'll be too late because I'm not sure if they'll let us take our oxygen and colostomy bags on the plane."

"Wait, what?"

Oh right, I guess I owed her a little backstory before I got to the colostomy bags.

Ultimately, though, she didn't require much persuasion. This was a chapter of our stories we would write together. "Okay," she said. "Let's make it happen."

I was trying to suck the marrow out in some ways. *But what does it look like to suck out the marrow, spiritually speaking?* I wondered. Whenever I considered the question, a seemingly paradoxical idea kept popping into my head: fasting. I couldn't quite make the connection. If I wanted to get the most out of life, that would mean tasting and seeing that the Lord was good, right?

Then I came across some musings by a fourth-century Christian bishop named Asterius, who said fasting ensures that the stomach will not make the body boil like a kettle to the hindering of the soul.[5] According to author Richard Foster, fasting, more than any other spiritual practice, reveals the things that control us. "We cover up what is inside us with food and other good things, but in fasting these things surface."[6]

It's not that food is inherently bad; it's that there's something, or rather someone, inherently better.

Maybe depriving myself of one of my physical senses would sharpen my spiritual senses somehow. And maybe the hunger pangs would point me to deeper hungers—the soul-level needs I was covering up with what I put in my mouth. Maybe fasting would help me determine what real marrow was in the first place.

There was just one problem: I felt downright panicky about going without food for more than a couple of hours. I was the kind of person who needed a morning snack, an afternoon snack, and a bedtime snack in addition to three round meals a day. And the simple truth was, I loved food. Aside from a high school fundraiser when we went without food and got ourselves hyped up on Mountain Dew to keep us going all night, I'd never fasted before. It sounded like something for people way more spiritual than an amateur like me.

But the idea wouldn't go away, so I finally conceded to an experiment of sorts. I'd fast once a week and focus my prayers on my One Big Request: that a good man would pursue me. I'd set aside every Thursday until my thirtieth birthday as a fast day. I wasn't sure exactly what I was expecting by putting a deadline on things, but it did seem like a convenient setup for God to work in. Wouldn't it just be *neat* if I made this act of sacrifice and then he, in turn, blessed me with a man in the nick of time (i.e., before I reached old maid status)?

It didn't take many Thursdays, however, to realize that the whole point of fasting was to divest myself of my own plans and surrender to what God was doing. Every hunger pang was a reminder that this was about God, not about me. God could listen to me just as well when my stomach was full as when it was empty; clearly this was more about getting my attention than about getting his.

∽

One evening a few months into my experiment, I got a phone call from Sarah. "What would you think about being in Venice with Seth and me for your thirtieth birthday?"

After a fair amount of the kind of squealing reserved for former roommates, we pulled out our calendars and our budgets, trying to figure out how to see Italy on a shoestring. We found a steal on the airline tickets and dug around online until we found out-of-the-way places we could rent for cheap. One woman who rented out rooms of her home in Florence promised "absolute relax moments" on the back patio. We were sold.

But there was one thing still nagging at me. "Will it be weird for me to be the third wheel?" I asked. When Sarah and I had daydreamed about visiting Italy in our college days, I guess I'd always assumed that it would be an even-numbered adventure. This scenario of my being the odd one out was something I hadn't anticipated.

But Sarah and Seth both assured me it would be fine.

I wrote the dates on my calendar. *Hmm*, I thought. *My birthday falls on a Thursday this year.* I couldn't think of a better way to break my fast than with a slice of authentic Italian pizza.

The Time Dad Pulled a Laban

I WAS ALMOST EIGHT when my sister was born, and from the moment she entered the world, Meghan spent every ounce of her energy trying to close the age gap between us. As soon as she could walk, she attempted to break out of the front door in the mornings to follow my brother and me onto the school bus. She begged Mom to enroll her in gymnastics, piano, basketball, and track—all the activities I was involved in—while she was still in diapers. When she was in preschool she pleaded with Mom to let her drink coffee. By the time she was in kindergarten, she was staging bedtime boycotts, refusing to put her head on the pillow until the big kids turned in. When it was time for me to go to college, she jokingly confiscated my admissions mail, trying to blackmail me into waiting eight years so we could enroll at the same time.

By the time I was a junior in college, though, Meghan was starting to come to terms with having me out of the house. She'd come and spend weekends in the dorm with me, and all my friends would treat her like one of the college girls. (I should mention, however, that the first night she spent in my dorm room, she was so excited she threw up in the hall bathroom. But that detail notwithstanding, the visit was a smashing success.) Then the summer after my junior year, I started dating a guy, and suddenly Meghan felt the pang of the age gap more sharply than ever.

I was staying at home with my parents for the summer, and Meghan had bound me to a strict agreement that I would wake her up when I got home from my dates, no matter what time it was. We conveniently failed to disclose our little arrangement to Mom, knowing she would have frowned on midnight wake-up calls for her twelve-year-old.

On one of those summer nights, I stopped into Meghan's room before brushing my teeth, and I could instantly tell something was on her mind.

"Do you like him?" There was an urgency to her voice that I couldn't quite nail down.

"Yeah, I like him," I said.

"No, do you really *like* him?" Her pitch was escalating, and I worried that Mom would find us out.

I hugged her. "Go to sleep," I whispered. "Let's talk tomorrow, okay?"

She grabbed my arm, begging me not to leave. "I know what's going to happen," she said, a quiver in her voice. "He's going to ask you to marry him and you're going to say yes and you're going to move away and have your own family and I'll still be here."

She was whisper-crying now.

"Aww, sweetie, don't worry. That's not going to happen right away."

Meghan's face suddenly got serious. "I want you to make me a promise."

"Sure. What is it?"

"When you get engaged, you have to tell me first. Before anyone else. Promise?"

I smiled at my sister, this four-foot bundle of determination and fierce love and freckles and gold-streaked hair. "Okay," I said. "I promise. But only if you promise the same thing back."

A giggle escaped amid her tears. "Yeah, right," she said. "That won't be until *forever*."

Still, we sealed our promise with a hug and reminded each other to act chipper and awake the next morning so Mom wouldn't be the wiser about our past-curfew activities. (We found out some years later that *of course* Mom had known all along.)

Within the span of a few months, the boyfriend and I had broken up, but the promise remained. I just never thought my baby sister would make good on her end of the deal before I did.

One night over a family dinner when Meghan's boyfriend, Ted, was visiting, my dad said he had an announcement to make. We all liked Ted, and by now it had become clear to everyone that Ted would be sticking around.

Based on Dad's trademark prankster tone, I had a pretty good hunch he was aiming to push somebody's buttons.

"I just came up with a great idea," he boomed. "I'm going to pull a Laban!"

My sister raised her eyebrows in his direction, and Ted eyed his proximity to the nearest exit. Where was Dad going with this?

He forged ahead, gaining momentum despite the apprehensive looks around the table. "I figure if we can get Ted to work for me to get Meghan, imagine the other possibilities!"

It was true that Ted had been helping Mom and Dad around the house all weekend—cleaning out the gutters, staining the deck, clearing dishes from the table.

Dad turned to me with his impish grin. "You know what that means, don't you? It means you can marry Ted too! This makes you . . . Leah!"

My dad isn't exactly Mr. Sensitivity, but he is a good man, and I knew he loved me. And I'm pretty sure he was more focused on the Laban angle of his ingenious plan—getting fourteen years of free labor. But even so, being cast as Leah in this drama felt less than flattering.

Leah, the older, less beautiful sister.

Leah, the undesired one.

Leah, who wasn't loved.

Leah, the second pick.

When my sister was finishing her last year of physical therapy school, she was assigned to a hospital not far from me, so we decided it made sense for her to live with me for the summer. Over the course of those few months, something interesting happened: The eight-year gap between us finally melted away. We discovered each other's quirks, as well as some of our own.

A few cases in point: Meghan refused to ask for help at Home Depot, even if we'd crossed the one-hour threshold on a mission to find whatever obscure hardware-related item we were looking for, whereas I made a beeline for the nearest friendly-looking face without blinking. When it was her turn to make dinner, she'd look in the fridge and throw something together sans recipe, while I was utterly lost without step-by-step directions from the kind people at allrecipes.com. She drove her car barefoot every day and simply left her work shoes in the car, while I was kind of obsessed with my three different shoe organizers.

We influenced each other in some surprising ways too. Although she never managed to convince me that peanuts taste better when you drink them straight from the jar, I had to admit that her morning cocktail suggestion of coffee mixed with peanut butter tasted better than I'd expected. In the mornings we ate breakfast together and found common ground in our mutual love of crossword puzzles. She'd gotten a gigantic, wall-sized crossword puzzle for college graduation, and we worked on it together each morning before work. She'd read the clues aloud, and I'd write the answers in the tiny boxes, wondering how we'd ever fill in all 10,000 answers. When we got home, we'd ride our bicycles together and regale each other with work stories over dinner (although I sometimes had to cut her off when she started getting into too much hospital-specific detail about what necrotic flesh smelled like and the process for debriding wounds).

One day near the end of Meghan's time with me, we decided to go on a bike ride despite the dark patch of clouds in the distance.

"I'm sure they'll blow over," Meghan said with a shrug. I nodded in agreement, and we hopped on our bikes.

About an hour from home we decided to turn around, and in that instant we knew we were doomed. The clouds that had been far off in the distance were no longer individual puffs of gray. Now there was a line clearly demarcated in the sky: cheery blue on one side and ominously black in the direction we were headed. Within a matter of minutes, the sky opened—not in individual droplets, but as a solid sheet of water.

And there we were, on a path that wound through the grounds of a small private airport—meaning there wasn't a single shelter or house in sight.

"What should we do?" Meghan shouted to me above the pelting water. "I can't see a thing!"

"Well, I'm pretty sure no one else is stupid enough to be out here. At least we won't run into anyone."

So we put our heads down and pedaled as hard as we could, despite soppy shoes and rain-smeared glasses.

By the time we arrived back at my house, the rain had let up, and improbably, the sun was starting to peek out from behind the clouds. We were drenched down to our underwear, and our socks squished with each step. But we couldn't stop giggling as we recounted our adventure with equal parts sheepishness and pride.

As we stood there dripping in my driveway, grinning like fools, Meghan suddenly pointed up into the sky.

I sucked in my breath. Not one rainbow but *two*. Both of them complete, arching from one end of the sky to the other.

I thought back to the day of Meghan's baptism years ago, when a double rainbow had graced the sky to mark the occasion. I remembered Mom standing at the window with Meghan, wiping tears from her eyes.

"Why are you crying, Mom?" I'd asked her.

"It feels like a promise," she said. "Like God is reminding us of his faithfulness."

As I stood there with Meghan, counting down the days until it was time for her to head back to grad school several states away, I knew things would never be quite like this again. She'd graduate, and if my hunch was correct, Ted would propose, and we'd never again live in the same house making dinner and going to Home Depot and doing giant crosswords together. Rachel would go on, and Leah would remain behind.

Suddenly, without my permission, the tears were dripping down my face, mingling with what was already a mess of rain and smeary mascara.

Meghan looked over at me, surprised.

"I guess I'm not ready for you to leave." My voice cracked.

She squished over to me and gave me an awkward hug around our bikes. "I thought of a way for us to keep doing crosswords in the mornings," she said. "I'll copy a part of the puzzle for you, and we can do it together over the phone."

It sounded like just the kind of thing two sisters might pull off. As we stood there taking in one last look at the double rainbow, it felt like one of those big promises. Like God was reminding us of his faithfulness. I had the rainbow—and the sister—to prove it.

⤮

A few months later my phone rang on a Saturday morning—suspiciously early.

Meghan!

I grabbed it on the first ring, and it was all I could do not to answer with "Did you say yes?"

Sure enough, she'd kept her promise—the one she'd made through tears way back in sixth grade. I was the first person she called. Neither of us would have dreamed it would happen quite like this . . . that she'd be the first to have a ring on her finger, the first to say "I do." And that when she fulfilled her promise to tell me, I'd be the one crying.

As I hung up the phone, my throat thick with joy and loss, something struck me: Meghan had called me first. I was her first choice.

I decided it was time to crack open my Bible and get the entire scoop on Leah and Rachel. In this account that would rival an afternoon soap, the sisterly competition didn't end in the jockeying for Jacob's affection; after that came the race to see which wife could give him more sons. And when the whole clan headed back to Jacob's homeland to meet up with the brother Jacob was convinced wanted to kill him, we get the idea that Leah was still Jacob's second choice, despite the fact that her scorecard boasted more sons. As they traveled toward Esau and his tribe, Jacob sent his family out in four groups, not coincidentally saving his first choice for the back of the entourage. Leah's servant and her servant's sons were sent to the front lines, followed by Rachel's servant and her children. Leah and her brood were next, while Jacob preserved his beloved Rachel and her sons for the very back.

As the Bible traces the lives of Jacob and his twelve sons, it's clear that he continued to show preferential treatment, even after Rachel died. Rachel's son Joseph got the best gifts and the most love from Dad, and after Joseph was presumed dead, Rachel's second son, Benjamin, became Jacob's sole reason for living. But for all the heroic tales of Joseph in Egypt, and for all that Rachel and her boys were Jacob's first choice, I noticed something a bit shocking when I combed through those tedious genealogies in the New Testament.

As it turns out, the line of the Messiah isn't traced back to Joseph, firstborn of Rachel, with his impressive résumé and leadership skills. Nor does the lineage come from Rachel's son Benjamin, the baby who cost Jacob's first choice her life in childbirth. No, the ancestor of Jesus was Judah. The son of Leah. In other words, Leah might not have been Jacob's first choice, but she was someone's first choice.

Whether or not I would ever be a man's first choice, I could, by some miracle, be God's first choice. Unlike humans, he has room in his heart for multiple first choices. And while I couldn't control whether I was Leah, I could control what my relationship with Rachel was like. I wanted our sisterhood to be marked not by competition but by grace. And maybe even an occasional coffee swirled with peanut butter.

Meghan's wedding was a perfect reflection of her and Ted—a simple affair where the bride and groom played horseshoes in their wedding attire before the ceremony. Meghan wore a simple white sundress and two braids in her hair—and of course, she went barefoot. I wore two braids out of a sense of sisterly loyalty and compromised on the footwear with a pair of flip-flops.

Sure enough, during the "giving-away" portion of the ceremony, when the pastor asked my dad to say a few words, he broke the ice with a crack about Rachel and Leah, reiterating his offer to Ted before going on to say nice fatherly things about Meghan and welcoming Ted to the family. But something was different this time.

Contrary to all the reactions I might have expected, I laughed. Not a self-pitying laugh or a bitter laugh. But a real, genuine belly laugh. One that likely would have made Leah jealous.

Parachute Prayers

OUR YEAR WAS UP.

Mason and I had originally agreed to pray for one year under our "Be annoying" motto. It was the last Tuesday of the year, and it was time to make a decision.

"So . . . do you think we should keep meeting?" Mason asked me.

I thought back over the year. In one sense our Tuesdays had been hard, especially articulating my deepest desires in their raw, unedited form—to myself, to God, and to a live human being. It had been uncomfortable to let my heart be exposed like that. And to top it all off, our little prayer experiment hadn't "worked." A year had passed, and neither of us was any closer to wedded bliss.

I agreed with Henri Nouwen's description of prayer as "no easy matter." He says that prayer "demands a relationship in which you allow someone other than yourself to enter into the very center of your person, to see there what you would rather leave in darkness, and to touch there what you would rather leave untouched."[1]

So why go back for more knocking around in the darkness? How long do you have to be annoying before you realize you're just beating your head against concrete?

The haunting promise from Scripture echoed in my ears: "Take delight in the LORD, and he will give you your heart's desires" (Psalm 37:4). God certainly didn't seem to be ceding any ground when it came to making good on that promise. Was it because I wasn't keeping my end of the bargain somehow? Was there some kind of divine loophole I was missing? Was God breaking his promise? Or was my desire wrong or misguided somehow?

I looked out the window at the scene that had magically transformed the world overnight. The first snowstorm of the season had burst through with white fury the evening before, turning the roads into a wintry Slip 'N Slide. But this morning there was only a spotless blanket covering every inch of the world, and with it the kind of peaceful hush that can be felt only from the muting effect of a fresh snowfall.

I marveled at how the snow clung to even the tiniest branch of every tree . . . how every ugly, dead thing was now pristine and beautiful. The same landscape I'd seen out my window the day before—drab and lifeless—had suddenly become a worthy desktop background. Everything was exactly the same: the same trees, the same ground, the same buildings. But everything looked completely different with this covering.

As I thought back over the year, in one sense, nothing had changed. But in another sense, everything had.

What if the measure of whether our yearlong experiment had "worked" was what had changed on the inside, not on the outside? By that standard, while the circumstances had remained the same, the internal landscape was as different as the snowy scene out my window. I hadn't arrived at any of the destinations I was hoping for—a man's love, marriage, a family—but I felt myself growing along the way. Although it still felt like I was taking a lot of steps in the dark, it didn't feel as scary as it used to. And I had to admit, at times I was even enjoying this journey, as different as it was from the one I'd thought I was setting out on.

This is how Julian of Norwich described God's response to our desires: "I am the ground of your beseeching. First, it is my will that you should have it, and then I make you to wish it, and then I make you to beseech it. If you beseech it, how could it be that you would not have what you beseech?"[2] For the first time that verse from Psalm 37 made sense. If God planted the desires in my heart in the first place, of course he'd give them to me.

Now I just needed to figure out which of the desires growing in me had been planted there by God and which were weeds.

My dad's parents were about to celebrate their sixtieth anniversary. I tried to get my brain around that number. Six decades of life spent with the same person. Almost three-quarters of their lives.

They'd been through so much together in those sixty years. Twelve children. An army of grandchildren. Even some great-grandchildren now. There had been times when the ends barely met and Grandma had to get creative so the kids would have clothes on their backs and food on the table. Grandpa had returned home in one piece from one war, and they'd narrowly missed having to send their six boys off to another. There had been ER trips, illnesses, and health scares, including Grandpa's recent stroke. Yet through it all they'd been faithful. To their God, to their family, to each other.

For their fiftieth anniversary, Grandma and Grandpa had returned to the same hotel where they'd stayed on their honeymoon. Sure enough, it was still standing—and Grandpa still had his receipt from five decades before. He brought the original bill to the desk, remembering what a stretch $26 had been in 1946 and hoping to get the same rate fifty years later. The manager had been surprised by his request but had ultimately agreed to a compromise: one dollar for each year they'd been married. Grandpa smiled smugly, knowing his wit and conscientiousness had paid off once again.

Now, ten years later, their situation looked a lot different. Grandpa was recovering from his stroke more successfully than anyone expected, but he was no longer the savvy, in-charge businessman he once was, and he and Grandma wouldn't be traveling across the country anytime soon.

Still, the occasion was worthy of celebrating. So the local relatives all gathered on the evening of their anniversary to mark the occasion and to say thanks for the years, thanks for the faithfulness, thanks for this big family they'd founded and chaired over these decades.

At some point in the evening someone pulled out the lone wedding photograph of my grandmother, beautiful and wide-eyed in her elegant silk gown. I'd always loved that picture, imagining her preparing for a simple church wedding as quickly as she could after Grandpa returned from World War II. According to church rules, they couldn't get married during Lent, and they certainly didn't want to wait an extra six weeks, so they squeezed in the ceremony on an otherwise ordinary Tuesday morning. But it wasn't until that evening that I heard the story of the dress.

Grandma told us that since silk was needed overseas for the war effort, it was extremely hard to come by in the 1940s. But my grandmother, spunky woman that she is, remained undeterred as she planned her wedding. She wrote a letter to her fiancé requesting that he send a used parachute from Europe so she could have it made into a dress.

Sure enough, the package of white silk arrived, and under the seamstress's deft fingertips, the object that had once been a symbol of war and tragedy was transformed into something new and beautiful.

I tried to imagine the emotions that must have flooded Grandma as she opened that package during her final year of college. Nothing would erase the difficulties Grandpa had experienced in the war—the deaths he felt responsible for, the buddies who didn't come home, the missions he shouldn't have survived. And nothing would take away the pain of Grandma's years of waiting as she worried and prayed over his safe return.

God didn't magically take all that pain away. But somehow all those memories got stitched together into the fabric of the silk parachute as they began their new life together. The token of what had separated them was transformed into a resplendent dress, a tangible sign of their love.

∿

At the end of the evening, after I said my good-byes to my relatives and hugged Grandma even more tightly than usual, I went home, doing futile math about how old I'd be if I ever managed to be married as long as my grandparents.

But in the back of my mind, something was nagging me about the parachute and our Tuesday prayers. What if this season I was in wasn't just something to get through, to survive? What if the point of praying wasn't just to get the answer I wanted, but to become the person God wanted me to be?

Maybe God wanted to take my sorrows and my failures and my longings and my dashed hopes and weave those threads together, transforming them into a beautiful garment for me to wear. Whether that dress would be white one day or not.

In the Desert

I LOOKED AROUND Ruth's living room, usually immaculate but now a wasteland of boxes and packing tape. I paused in the middle of wrapping one of Ruth's delicate glass dishes.

We were sorting all her earthly treasures into three different boxes: "To be moved," "To be given away," and "?" I couldn't believe how much had changed in such a short time. Only months ago, Ruth and Bob had been healthy, independent, self-sufficient. Now Ruth was trapped in an immobilizing neck cast and Bob was fading in and out of reality like a distant radio station.

When I peeked inside the giveaway box and saw so many classic Ruth belongings—things she'd entertained with and decorated her home with for decades, including items I recalled from that memorable snow-day visit all those years ago—I could hardly hold it together. On a practical level, it was a sensible time for Ruth and

Bob to move into an assisted-living facility. But how could she keep herself from crumbling under the grief and loss of it all?

"How can you do this, Ruth?" I finally asked, my eyes misting despite my best efforts to be strong for her sake.

"Well, one thing I've learned over all these years is to be present in the moment," she said. "No amount of moping is going to take me back to how things used to be. And no amount of wishing is going to change the future."

After a pause she said, "Have I ever told you about how Bob and I decided to get married?"

I shook my head, and she motioned for me to join her on the couch.

She and Pastor Bob had celebrated their anniversary just a few weeks before. "Sixty-one years," she said, her eyes sparkling. Her face became animated as she recounted the story of their whirlwind engagement. The two of them had dated for a few years, having attended the same country school in South Dakota, with just twenty-two people in their graduating class.

Bob had known for some time that he wanted to marry her, but he didn't want to propose until he was sure he could provide for her and a family. It was just after World War II, and housing was scarce. But then one day his father spotted a deal on some nearby acreage and asked Bob to farm it for him. Bob didn't hesitate. He rushed straight to Ruth's third-floor apartment, taking the stairs three at a time. "We can get married!" he told her.

"When?" Ruth asked, surprised.

"How about in two weeks?" He was fairly bursting with boyish elation.

That sounded a little fast to Ruth. "No, I can't do that to my mother," Ruth said. "Let's make it three weeks."

Ruth broke out of her reverie with a laugh. "Only three weeks to plan a wedding—and just before Christmas, at that!"

Then a shadow came over her cheery countenance. "I married a man," she said, "and now he's turning into a little boy."

Ruth leaned back into the couch as far as she could with the neck brace in the way. "All change—even good change—is accompanied by the pains of childbirth."

When I looked at her quizzically, she continued. "Although I loved Bob and believed it was God's will for us to get married, the transition came with its pangs. It meant leaving a job I enjoyed as a designer for Montgomery Ward—a pretty unusual position for women in the 1940s. And then when we set sail for Brazil, we had to say good-bye to my parents, knowing it might mean we'd never see them again, that they'd likely never meet the rest of their grandchildren." Ruth's voice trailed off, and I got the sense that her heart was now somewhere in 1952.

As we sat on the couch, both lost in thoughts of our own, I thought about a poem by seventeenth-century Japanese poet and samurai Mizuta Masahide. It's startlingly short—the title is half the poem—but it's all the more poignant for its simplicity.

BARN'S BURNT DOWN
Barn's burnt down—
now
I can see the moon.

Would I see only tragedy when life didn't turn out the way I'd planned? Or would I let my burned-down dreams give me a new perspective?

Finally Ruth continued her story. "When we left Brazil, there was the pain of leaving friends we'd become close to over the past ten years—not to mention the pain of not knowing what would happen with the ministry we'd invested so much of our lives in."

"And what about now?" I asked hesitantly.

"Now we are going through another change, another childbirth. In order to get to the new beginning, we have to go through the pain of this season ending."

There was no way she could have known it then, but within the span of a year, as Bob's mental health declined, her neck would heal, and she'd no longer need the brace—just as she had predicted. The doctor never said the word *miracle*; he just shook his head in disbelief, telling all who would listen: "I have no explanation for what happened. But I can't take any credit for this."

For now, though, all she knew was that her barn was burning down. Yet all she saw was the moon.

Everywhere I turned in the weeks after my visit with Ruth, I kept stumbling on a distinctively odd theme: deserts. These dry places jumped out at me from the pages of Scripture—Moses wandering the desert for forty years before God got his attention in the form of a fiery bush, Isaiah promising a day when God would bring streams of water gushing through the wasteland, Jesus being tempted in the desert before he began his official marching orders as Messiah.

I'd also been spending some time reading about the desert fathers and mothers, who, true to their name, had quite an affinity for the wilderness. The way they came to be known as people of the desert is fascinating in itself. It was the third century AD, and the persecution that had plagued Christians for hundreds of years had finally lifted. For the first time in the history of the Roman Empire, it was safe to be a Christian. After an era marked by torture and martyrdom, those who followed Jesus were being welcomed into society.

You'd think that on the heels of such persecution, Christ followers would have basked in their newfound freedom and the comfort of being able to live their lives in peace. But shockingly, it was out of that positive cultural shift that the monastic movement was born. The desert fathers and mothers went into the Egyptian wilderness not to avoid a difficult situation but to avoid one that was too comfortable.

It was with these whispers from the desert swirling in my ears that I stumbled on the heart-wrenching story of Hosea and his relentless love for his wife, Gomer. Though this couple may not have lived in a literal desert, Gomer's unfaithfulness made their marriage as barren and parched as any wasteland. She cheated on him again and again, but he kept taking her back, pursuing her and wooing her, knowing even as he did that she'd reject him for lesser loves as soon as the next opportunity presented itself.

The story struck me as outrageous, flying in the face of everything I deemed just and right and fair. I found myself wanting to shout some sense into Hosea across the centuries: *Why would a nice guy like you keep taking back this woman who is clearly not good enough for you?* But I wasn't too far into the story before it became clear that this wasn't just an account about a long-dead prophet. It was about how God's people have "acted like a prostitute by turning against the Lord and worshiping other gods" (Hosea 1:2).

That cheating woman was me.

I'd found true love in God, yet I consistently gave my heart to unworthy substitutes: Comfort. Security. Dreams that were limited to this world. The approval of others. That ever-elusive ideal of the man I was looking for. People and things that weren't meant to step into the role only God could fill in my heart.

But that's where the beautiful part came in. Hosea didn't wait for his fickle bride to return to him, groveling for forgiveness. No, he pursued her, using every courting trick in the book to win her back. And God does the same for his people, for his bride. For me.

The Lord says:

I will win her back once again.
  I will lead her into the desert
  and speak tenderly to her there.

HOSEA 2:14

At first the desert struck me as an odd choice for wooing. It doesn't have quite the romantic appeal of, say, a candlelight dinner or a walk along the beach. Why would God do his courting in the desert?

But the more I thought about it, the more I wondered if the desert fathers were onto something. Maybe when you're in the wilderness, it's easier to have an honest talk about your relationship. In the desert, after all, life moves at a slower pace. You have limited creature comforts. Less noise. Fewer distractions. And maybe then, in the uncomfortable quiet, you can sit down and really talk. Maybe then you can pause long enough to hear the words your beloved is tenderly speaking to you.

Abba Cronius, one of the desert fathers, put it this way: "If the soul is vigilant and withdraws from all distraction and abandons its own will, then the spirit of God invades it."[1]

And I wondered: *What if the desert isn't a punishment after all? What if the desert is a place where I could finally make room for the one who loved me so he could invade my heart, my soul?*

What if the desert was actually the best place to be wooed?

Ruth's words about the pain of childbirth kept popping into my head at random moments—while I was brushing my teeth, while I was stuck in traffic, while I was zoning out in work meetings. I found the image strangely comforting. I'd felt for some time like something was gradually changing, like my internal tectonic plates were shifting. My circumstances looked pretty much the same, and I certainly hadn't experienced anything as drastic as a broken neck or a move out of polite society and into the desert. It was more like something was changing *inside* me.

All along I'd vaguely assumed the emptiness and the pain meant I was doing something wrong. But maybe it was all just part of the process so something new could be born. First the barrenness, to make space. Then the pain, which is the only way to a birth.

Maybe something was being born after all. Something was being born in me.

The Big 3-0

PLAN TO GET LOST IN VENICE. That theme kept recurring as Sarah and Seth and I made the itinerary for our trip, and I wasn't quite sure what to make of it.

Whenever I talked to people who had visited there while in Italy, this recurring bit of advice (or warning, depending on the source) kept echoing in my ears. It was a bit disturbing for a planner like me. I enjoyed the process of figuring out what to do, when to do it, and what the backup would be in case my arrangements didn't work out. I might not have had a stellar internal compass, but if I pinned everything down ahead of time, I felt confident I could find my way around. But planning to get lost? That wasn't on my to-do list for our long-anticipated week in Italia.

We stepped out of the train station in Venice, bleary eyed and exhausted after traveling the better part of the day—first by plane and then by train, having sustained ourselves with catnaps and a sufficient supply of airline peanuts. Now we were finally here. In Italy. In Venice.

My first glimpse of the floating city—under the glow of street lamps and the full moon—was every bit as magical as I'd dreamed it would be. I couldn't stop exclaiming over the roads that were paved with water, the taxis that came in the form of ornate black-and-red gondolas, the smells of baking bread on every corner, the artists painting scenes of the city with oils and watercolors.

The next day—our first full day in Venice and also my birthday—the three of us found ourselves sitting on a bench overlooking Venice's Grand Canal. We were savoring our second chocolate-hazelnut gelato of the day and deciding how to spend our final hours in the city. Recharged by the sugar boost, we pulled out our guidebook to create a plan.

So far, we'd dutifully stuck to our trusty book and followed the signs posted for tourists. Sure, on a few occasions we'd unwittingly taken the long way around and had to backtrack a street or two, but we'd managed to avoid getting truly turned around. We'd already visited Venice's must-sees—the Duomo with its intricate stone carvings, the Piazza with its legendary pigeons, the palace with its storied Bridge of Sighs. We'd come to this floating city with high expectations of its art and history and culture, and Venice hadn't disappointed.

But what about the admonitions about getting lost? I wondered if we were missing something. And so, sitting on that bench, the three of us made a pact: That afternoon we'd toss the guidebook (or at least put it at the bottom of a backpack) and plan to lose ourselves in Venice. Besides, since Venice is essentially an island, we figured we couldn't wind up too far off course. Still, I felt naked without my trusty Frommer's in hand.

But as we embarked on the mapless segment of our Venetian adventure, we encountered off-the-path delights we never could have known without getting lost. Each time we turned a corner, we were presented with an unexpected new sight. A cobblestone alley weaving in unlikely patterns through residential areas, only to dead-end abruptly at a quaint stone wall. A gray-haired woman leaning out a third-story window to hang her laundry and call to a neighbor across the street. A little courtyard where a dozen children in blue school uniforms were kicking around a "football."

We turned a corner at the end of one street and were surprised to see the cobblestone path open into a trellised walkway covered with purple flowers. It wasn't a scene that would have made it into any guidebook, but maybe that was part of its magic. I stooped down and picked up a small rock from the pathway. I wanted a piece of Italy to take home with me. Another stone of remembrance.

When I'd embarked on my weekly fast leading up to my thirtieth birthday, I'm not entirely sure what I'd been expecting. I suppose at some level I saw it as a spiritual bargain of sorts—that if I fulfilled my end of the deal, God would respond by giving me what I wanted. Maybe somewhere in the back of my mind, I thought Mr. Fulfillment of My Heart's Desires would have made an appearance by the time the big 3-0 rolled around.

Truth be told, I was looking for the guidebook in my regular life too. All this time I'd been presenting my itineraries to God, hoping he'd let me map everything out. But sitting along a canal in Venice, I was reminded that life doesn't come with a guidebook—and God certainly won't be confined to the likes of a Frommer's. What adventures would I miss out on, I wondered, if I stayed on the predictable, well-marked paths I'd planned out for myself? Maybe he had plans for me off the main drag, where beautiful and unexpected surprises bloomed amid the twisting, turning back alleys.

I officially broke my weekly fast at a restaurant right on the water, and as I sat there with my two friends, savoring gnocchi with cream sauce, I wondered if Venice proved that love at first sight is possible after all.

This wasn't what I'd been praying for. I was still as single as ever, the third wheel in the most romantic city in the world. But something remarkable had happened: I was thirty and single, and the world hadn't imploded. I was thirty and single, and I was in Italy eating out-of-this-world cuisine with my friends. I was thirty and single, and God was still who he said he was. I was thirty and single, and I was going to be okay.

After nine months of fasting and prayer, God hadn't changed my circumstances. He'd changed *me*.

"Here's to Venezia," I said.

"To thirty," Seth said.

"To friends," Sarah said.

I thought of the last poem in T. S. Eliot's *Four Quartets*:

The end of all our exploring
Will be to arrive where we started
And know the place for the first time.

As I gazed out at the canal just inches from our dinner table, I whispered another silent toast. *Here's to abundant life, to sucking out the marrow. And here's to throwing away the map.*

Here's to getting lost.

Last Blind Date

WHEN A COWORKER stopped by my office to chat that afternoon, I didn't suspect anything unusual at first. It was her hands that gave her away. She couldn't quite figure out what to do with them, and they just seemed to be getting in the way. Then I noticed that each time the conversation seemed to be wrapping up, she'd come up with some non sequitur to keep her firmly seated on the chair in my office. Finally I couldn't take the suspense any longer.

"Did you want to ask me something? Whatever it is, it's okay."

Her hands clasped together, seemingly happy to have found an occupation. "Oh, thank you," she said. "Um, I was wondering if, well . . . if you'd be open to being set up."

Internally I groaned. It had been years since I'd been on a blind date. I was in my thirties now. Too old for setups. I'd tried that route, and it just hadn't worked for me. I had eight rocks in my little fabric bag to prove it.

But how could I tell that to this woman who was wringing her hands like the world was going to end as she awaited my reply?

I agreed, under one unspoken condition. *This would be my last blind date.* I said as much to Sarah when I filled her in on the few details I knew: Apparently this guy was the roommate of my coworker's boyfriend, he worked with special needs students, and he enjoyed riding his bicycle. And he liked peanut butter more than anyone else she knew.

Sarah, ever more hopeful than I, thought it sounded auspicious. "After all, you like peanut butter too," she pointed out.

But with those eight previous flops on my mind, I had a more statistically sound perspective.

"I'll give him a chance," I said. "But I have no delusions this will be any different from the others. You heard it right now—this is it. My last blind date."

ربی

Daniel and I agreed to meet on the bike path near my house on a June afternoon. He'd e-mailed me a map and identified the spot where he'd be. I told him I'd be the one in the pink shirt.

As I rode down a steep wooden switchback under a drizzling sky, I was fretting about a dozen things on constant repeat. Would he be there yet? What would we talk about? Would I be interrogated about my theological beliefs? Would there be a marriage-material checklist I had to pass? Would I have to carry the conversation while he looked utterly bored? And what on earth was my hair doing under my helmet with the added insult of the frizz-inducing mist? Maybe I should just turn around now and forget this crazy idea altogether.

But before I had the chance to chicken out, a man matching my coworker's description popped up from where he was sitting beside the trail.

"You must be Stephanie," he said.

We fell into conversation quickly, and it was several minutes before I realized my helmet was still firmly strapped to my chin. Not exactly the glamorous first impression I'd envisioned, but my date didn't seem to mind. Daniel and I found out we had a lot in common—his dad was one of thirteen children, and my dad was one of twelve. Our moms both had accounting backgrounds and taught Bible studies at their church. We each had one sister and one brother. We'd both had jobs in education. And those were the discoveries we made in just the first five minutes.

Daniel looked at the sky thoughtfully. "What do you think? Should we try to take a bike ride, or should we go with the backup plan?"

Backup plan? I was impressed already.

"I don't think it will rain." I felt confident. "Let's go for it."

He smiled. *Oh, what a nice smile.* "Okay," he said. "Why don't we head toward my car and then we'll be close just in case."

We hadn't been riding for more than two minutes when the sky opened up in a torrential rain. I locked up my bicycle as quickly as I could and then we both dove for cover in his car.

I looked over at Daniel through my smudged glasses, aware that my carefully straightened hair was a mess and that my mascara was probably running down my cheeks. Apparently I wouldn't be able to appear put together for even a fraction of this date.

But when we made eye contact, I saw that his blue eyes were dancing and that winsome smile of his was playing at the corners of his mouth. "Well, this will be a memorable date," he said.

I didn't know how all this would play out, but I was sure he was right about that. And not just for meteorological reasons, but because for the first time in my blind dating career, I felt like I could be completely myself with a man. It wasn't that there weren't any awkward moments, but I felt safe with him in the midst of the awkward.

As I headed home from the date on my bike, after a backup plan that included indoor roller skating, bowling, and—once the sun reappeared—a picnic of Daniel's homemade banana bread, I eyed the spot where I'd first seen him.

I came to a sudden stop when it hit me. I'd been so distracted by the thought of meeting him that I hadn't realized at first what had blocked Daniel from view on the side of the trail. He'd been behind a rock. A big old rock—solid and waist high, sitting regally along the path. Almost as if someone had it put there on purpose.

Like a stone of remembrance . . . one big enough that even someone as blind as I was could stumble upon it. And in the midst of the falling, to discover the grace that had been there all along.

Acknowledgments

THANKS TO MY AMAZING TEAM AT TYNDALE: to Sarah Atkinson and Jan Long Harris, for believing in this book (and me) from the beginning and for championing it all the way through; to Jillian, for shepherding me through this process with excellence and encouragement; to Sharon, for her faithful friendship and prayers; to Kim, for her thoughtful, wise edits; to Sarah and Annette, for their careful attention to detail; to Jackie, for the brilliant cover; to Nancy, Cassidy, Maggie, and Christy, for launching this book into the world; to Tim, for wrangling the schedule at every turn; and to the sales team, for making sure my mom isn't the only person who buys this book.

Thanks to everyone who has allowed me to share part of their lives on these pages. I'm honored that you'd let me tell your stories but most of all that I've had the privilege of living out our stories together.

Thanks to my amazing family—Mom and Dad, Kyle and Amber, Meghan and Ted, the Rische clan, and the smartest, cutest, most talented nieces and nephews in the world (based on purely objective standards). Thank you for always supporting me, coming to all my basketball games, and showing me what God's unconditional love looks like.

Thanks to the Sarahs, for being what I can only call my book-writing support group. Yours were the first eyes on this manuscript, and it's only because of you that this book ever went beyond the boundaries of my own brain. C. S. Lewis said that friendship is born that moment when one person says to another, "What! You too?" and I'm thankful for all the "What! Sarah too?" moments in my life.

Thanks to the Sister Southies, who prayed this book into existence, and to the Thursday prayer ladies, who have been a weekly rock all these years.

Thanks to the gifted teachers who taught me to write and to love words and books and language, especially Mrs. Dunn-Reier, Mr. Heagney, and Dr. Warren.

Thanks to all the matchmakers who set me up. Even when the match wasn't a success, I felt noticed and loved—and grateful that you would put yourself out there on my behalf. (And yes, Adam, we remember we still owe you.)

Thanks to Daniel, my last blind date ever. You are my Ephesians 3:20—more than I could have asked for or imagined. You were so worth the wait.

Most of all, thanks to God, who continues to shower me with more grace and love than I could ever deserve.

Discussion Guide

This study guide will help you further explore the themes of Stephanie's journey in *I Was Blind (Dating), but Now I See*. Grab a cup of coffee, break out the snacks, and invite others to join you—your girlfriends, your small group, your neighbors—or use this guide on your own for individual reflection. For more resources, visit www.StephanieRische.com.

PART 1: WAITING

1. Have you ever been on a blind date? What was it like to get set up? How did the date go?

2. Describe a season when you've felt like you were waiting on God. What were you waiting for? What made the waiting difficult? What were some ways that you stayed close to God while you were waiting?

3. Would you describe yourself as an impatient person? Who tests your patience? How do you work to grow your patience with your friends, your family, and God?

4. How does Stephanie's definition of Advent—a time of "holding your breath"—change your view of what it means to be in a waiting season? What are you holding your breath for right now?

PART 2: FAITHFULNESS

1. Have you ever been on a date with someone who "checks all the boxes" on your mental list of the kind of person you're looking for, but the chemistry isn't there? What happened?

2. After the boring date with The Professor, Stephanie makes a pro/con list of what qualities/strengths/weaknesses she brings to a relationship. Do you have a clear idea of who you are and what *you* bring to a relationship? What are some of your own strengths and weaknesses?

3. Do you believe that God loves you unconditionally, regardless of all your pros/cons? Why or why not?

4. Stephanie is unexpectedly accosted with dating advice by Dorothy, her well-intentioned friend. How do you handle the "Dorothys" in your life? How can we be supportive and accountable friends to each other without pressuring or implying blame?

5. Do you have a mentor? What are some qualities you would look for in a mentoring relationship? Does anyone specific come to mind whom you would consider asking to support you in this way?

6. Unexpectedly, Stephanie finds herself alone in the midst of the "Summer of Weddings." How do you gracefully navigate a season where you feel like everyone is moving forward without you?

PART 3: COMMUNITY

1. Do you know your neighbors? What fears may stop you from reaching out and making a connection?

2. After forming an unlikely friendship with Blanca, Stephanie remarks, "It wasn't the kind of community I'd been

looking for (i.e., a husband and a family of my own), but God, as usual, seemed to delight in surprising me." What communities have you stumbled into and found unexpected support from?

3. What is your definition of hospitality? What are some small steps you can take this week to provide a space for conversation and community?

4. Do you feel like you are putting your life on hold while you wait for the desire of your heart—whether that be a relationship, a job, or another dream? How can we be intentional in truly living, moving to get unstuck?

5. Stephanie says, "You can't embrace life if you don't dance at the edge of your fears." What's holding you back from a more abundant life?

PART 4: HOPE

1. Are statistics comforting or concerning to you? In what ways has God "beaten the odds" in your life?

2. What prayers have you prayed that seemed to "miscarry"? How do you cope and continue to hope when you feel your prayers are going unanswered? Are there ways we can support each other and remind each other of God's goodness in these times?

3. Stephanie remarks, "I knew what it was like to get my hopes up, only to have them shattered on the rocks of real life." Describe a time when you could relate to this sentence. How did you pick up the pieces of hope?

4. How can we honestly bring our disappointments to God without settling into resentment and bitterness?

PART 5: PRAYER

1. Have you ever been hurt by the church? What happened, and
    how did you move through it?

2. What do you do when your "people" get busy or shift priorities
    and it feels like you have no one to fall back on?

3. Stephanie recounts the story of Jacob and his wrestling match
    with the Lord, leaving Jacob with a permanent limp—"a tangible
    reminder of his encounter with a God who doesn't usually show
    up so tangibly." What are some of your reminder scars?

4. Have you ever had a prayer buddy? Who in your life could you
    approach with the "quest to become annoying"?

PART 6: GRATITUDE

1. On the scale of gratitude, where do you find yourself right
    now? What are some things that are limiting/helping your
    awareness of God's goodness?

2. What are some of the hindrances to your spiritual life? Are
    there any ideas that come to your mind to help you practice a
    deeper connection with him?

3. How has God broken your comforts, forcing you to look at the
    world in a whole new way?

4. How content would you say you are right now with where your
    life is? How do you deal with discontentment when it rears its
    head?

PART 7: JOY

1. Emily Dickenson says, "Forever—is composed of Nows." How can
    we slow down and work to be present and engaged in our Now?

2. How do you navigate "cross-life-stage friendships"? Are there ways we can be intentional with people who are not experiencing what we are?

3. What is so difficult about rejoicing with those who rejoice? How can we put aside our own struggles/triumphs to meet people where they are?

4. What are some of your "why" prayers?

PART 8: JOURNEY

1. Let's be honest—Stephanie's date with Limo Dude was pretty awkward. What is your worst date story?

2. Has God ever sent you a "double rainbow" reminder of his faithfulness?

3. Stephanie suggests that God does his courting of us in the desert seasons. How have you seen this truth in your own life?

4. Sometimes God takes us down paths in our journeys that we never would have chosen ourselves. How have you seen God's grace and love in the seasons when life didn't turn out the way you imagined?

Notes

SPIRITUAL BREATH HOLDING
1. Frederick Buechner, *Whistling in the Dark* (New York: Harper Collins, 1993), 3.

THE MANNA PRINCIPLE
1. John Chryssavgis, *In the Heart of the Desert: The Spirituality of the Desert Fathers and Mothers* (Bloomington, IN: World Wisdom, Inc.: 2003), 22-23.

THRICE A BRIDESMAID
1. "Faithful," Second Circle, Enter the Worship Circle (2001).
2. Mark Williams, "Miracle," *Journals of a Recovering Skeptic* (Awakening Records).

FOR SALE BY OWNER
1. Richard H. Schmidt, *God Seekers: Twenty Centuries of Christian Spiritualties* (Grand Rapids: William B. Eerdmans, 2008), 20.

ARE YOU MY NEIGHBOR?
1. Richard H. Schmidt, *God Seekers*, 52.
2. G. K. Chesterton, *Heretics* (Nashville: Sam Torode Book Arts, 2011), 80.
3. Ibid.

THE THEOLOGY OF HUCKLEBERRY PIE
1. See Matthew 26:17-30.

MOLE CHECKUPS AND OTHER FORMS OF ACCOUNTABILITY
1. Dietrich Bonhoeffer, *A Testament to Freedom* (New York: HarperOne, 2009), 27.
2. Dietrich Bonhoeffer, *Life Together* (New York: Harper & Row, 1954), 77.
3. John Chryssavgis, *In the Heart of the Desert: The Spirituality of the Desert Fathers and Mothers* (Bloomington, IN: World Wisdom, Inc.: 2003), 22-23.

GOD AND THE ODDS
1. Andy Butcher, "Churches Warned of Female Burnout," Beliefnet.com, http://www.beliefnet.com/News/2000/03/Churches-Warned-Of-Female-Burnout.aspx.
2. See Judges 7.

FEATHERS AND AXES
 1. Emily Dickinson, "Hope Is the Thing with Feathers," lines 1–2.
 2. Rebecca Solnit, *Hope in the Dark* (New York: Nation Books, 2004), 5.

FIGHTING MY DRAGONS ALONE
 1. All parties involved support the inclusion of this story.
 2. Selections from *The Sayings of the Desert Fathers*, translated by Benedicta Ward (Kalamazoo, MI: Cistercian Publications, 1975), 43.

MY QUEST TO BECOME ANNOYING
 1. *Book of Common Prayer* (New York: Church Publishing, 1979), 234.
 2. C. S. Lewis, *Letters to Malcolm* (New York: Harcourt, 1963), 53.

CONFESSIONS OF AN UNGRATEFUL HEART
 1. C. S. Lewis, *Letters to Malcolm*, 26.
 2. *The Liturgy of the Hours: Office of Readings*, from a Letter to Proba by Saint Augustine of Hippo, http://sojo.net/articles/voice-day-augustine-3.

FORTY DAYS OF UNCLOISTERED LIFE
 1. *The Sayings of the Desert Fathers*, translated by Benedicta Ward (Kalamazoo, MI: Cistercian Publications, 1975), 118.

CONTENTMENT, LIKE IT OR NOT
 1. Timothy Keller, *Counterfeit Gods* (New York: Dutton, 2009), 11, italics in original.

A DIVINE CANVAS
 1. Emily Dickinson, "Forever—Is Composed of Nows," in *The Poems of Emily Dickinson*, ed. R. W. Franklin (Cambridge, MA: Harvard University Press, 1999).

A FAMILY OF ONE
 1. Dietrich Bonhoeffer, *Life Together*, translated by J. W. Doberstein (London: SCM Press, 1954).

FULL OF GRACE
 1. See Luke 2:19, NIV.

WHEN JOY COMES IN CAMO
 1. Julian of Norwich, *The Life of the Soul: Showings*, edited by Kathleen A. Walsh, translated by Edmund Colledge and James Walsh (Mahwah, NJ: Paulist Press, 1966), 249.
 2. Augustine, *Confessions*, 1.6, quoted in Richard H. Schmidt, *God Seekers* (Grand Rapids, MI: Wm. B. Eerdmans Publishing Co., 2008), 54.

BONE-CRUSHING HAPPINESS
1. C. S. Lewis, *Surprised by Joy* (Orlando, FL: Harcourt, 1955).

SUCKING OUT THE MARROW
1. Henry D. Thoreau, *Walden* (New York: Thomas Y. Crowell and Co., 1910), 118.
2. Willa Cather, *O Pioneers!* (Boston: Houghton Mifflin Company, 1913), 286.
3. Ibid., 182.
4. Ibid., 307.
5. David R. Smith, *Fasting: A Neglected Discipline* (Fort Washington, PA: Christian Literature Crusade, 1969), 39.
6. Richard J. Foster, *Celebration of Discipline* (New York: HarperOne, 1998), 55.

PARACHUTE PRAYERS
1. Henri J. Nouwen, *With Open Hands* (Notre Dame, IN: Ave Maria Press, 1972), 19.
2. Julian of Norwich, *The Life of the Soul: Showings*, 248.

IN THE DESERT
1. *Selections from the Sayings of the Desert Fathers*, translated by Benedicta Ward (Kalamazoo, MI: Cistercian Publications, 1975), 115.

About the Author

STEPHANIE RISCHE is a retired serial blind dater who happily exchanged her final blind date for a husband. Since getting married, she has been reaping the benefits of having a live-in dishwasher emptier, a homemade ice cream concocter, and a humorist-in-residence. Several years into this marriage gig, Stephanie is still trying to learn the finer points of sharing the covers.

On any given day you are likely to find Daniel and Stephanie riding on the bike path near the river, playing Beatles cover songs on the guitar (Daniel), or clutching a book in one hand and a pen in the other (Stephanie).

Stephanie is a senior editor of nonfiction books at Tyndale House Publishers. She and Daniel live in the Chicago area with their seventeen houseplants and a minimum of four jars of peanut butter.

"That endless, exhausting crusade for approval? Ends here."
ANN VOSKAMP

LOVE IDOL

Letting go of
your need for approval
—and seeing yourself
through God's eyes

JENNIFER DUKES LEE
Foreword by Lisa-Jo Baker

978-1-4143-8073-5

YOU ARE PREAPPROVED!

WE ALL WANT TO BE VALUED, TO BE RESPECTED. TO BE LOVED.

Yet this yearning too often turns into an idol of one of God's most precious gifts: love itself. If you, like so many of us, spend your time and energy trying to earn someone's approval—at work, home, or church—all the while fearing that, at any moment, the facade will drop and everyone will see your hidden mess . . . then love may have become an idol in your life.

Join Jennifer Dukes Lee in *Love Idol*, a journey to dismantle what's separating you from true connection with God, and rediscover the astonishing freedom of a life lived in authentic love.

CP1028

Bring *Brave Enough* to your community, and start living

BOLD and FREE

Brave Enough

Find the courage to be who you are . . . not who you wish you were. Discover what it means to live a brave-enough life, fully alive and confident in who God made you to be.

978-1-4964-0136-6

Brave Enough DVD Group Experience

Join Nicole on an eight-week journey to being brave enough right where you are.

978-1-4964-0138-0